Chase the Wind

by
DEBORAH LAWRENCE
and
AGGIE VILLANUEVA

THOMAS NELSON PUBLISHERS
Nashville • Camden • New York

Published in Nashville, Tennessee, by Thomas Nelson, Inc. and distributed in Canada by Lawson Falle, Ltd., Cambridge, Ontario.

Printed in the United States of America.

Unless otherwise noted, the Bible verses in this book are taken from *The Living Bible* (Wheaton, Illinois: Tyndale House Publishers, 1971) and are used by permission.

Bible verses marked NKJV are from The New King James Version. Copyright © 1979, 1980, 1982, Thomas Nelson, Inc., Publishers.

Library of Congress Cataloging in Publication Data

Lawrence, Deborah.
  Chase the wind.

  1. Hosea, the Prophet—Fiction.   I. Villanueva, Aggie.
II. Title.
PS3562.A912C48   1983   813'.54   83-8125
ISBN 0-8407-5840-5

To El Shaddai, You've been more than enough.

To Bob and Tricia, who've given enough.

Debbie

To Eddie, my Hosea.

Aggie

ACKNOWLEDGMENTS

Thanks to
. . . our husbands, Bob and Eddie for their belief in us shown by the staggering stacks of dirty dishes they've washed, consenting to the consumption of cold meals and suffering through suppers they've prepared and consumed alone while we worked on The Book.
. . . our children, Eddie, Tricia, Nicky, and Angie for practicing premeditated praise.
. . . our friends, Marsha Befort and Mary Doolittle for resplendent responses and restrained rebuttals.
. . . our moms, Pat Crumby and Bobbie Barker, sis Linda Rogers, and friends Amy Berry and Phyllis Dugger for supplementary support.
. . . our friend Cathy Castaneda for the accidental introduction to Hosea.
. . . a sis-in-law from Arkansas, Linda Lemmons for her enormous enthusiasm and perpetual promotion.
. . . our writer friends, Tom Noton and Charlotte Adelsperger for diligent directives and precious prayers, and to another writer friend, Esther Vogt for her cure-all critique during a creative crisis.
. . . our editor, Lisa Ferris for her frankness, forbearance, and flawless finesse.
. . . associate pastor at Full Faith Church of Love, Jim Cox for the accuracy of the historical background note.
. . . owners of Glad Tidings Bookstore in Shawnee, Kansas, Ardy and Jerry Kolb for their considerate consignment of their reference books.
. . . photographer and real estate agent, Gary Meador of Texas, a sympathetic stranger who suspended a pilgrimage from Pampa to "fix our photos."
. . . our many other friends and acquaintances for all their aid.
And last but not least, we gratefully acknowledge each other.

These are the messages from the Lord to Hosea, son of Beeri, during the reigns of these four kings of Judah: Uzziah, Jotham, Ahaz, and Hezekiah; and one of the kings of Israel, Jeroboam, son of Joash.

Hosea 1:1

Prologue

By dawn, the mount of Beth-el had consumed the body of Diblaim and felt the weight of those who wept for him.

Professional mourners wove among the funeral procession as they left the tombs and climbed barefoot up the copper-colored soil of the mountainside. These skillful women with disheveled hair rent their clothes and streaked their faces with dirt, while chanting a siren song that conjured up grief among those who barely knew the departed Diblaim. To the accompaniment of a tinkling tambourine, their swaying, distorted limbs moved in a melancholy dance, and their dirge invoked the villagers to "weep with those who weep."

9

"Ah, Diblaim, who sat among the gates and counseled with the elders," one of the skillful women wailed. "We grieve the loss of you. Why have you deserted your family and friends? O, Beth-el, is there one who could take his place? How great is your name, Diblaim."

The woman's outburst prodded Salome, the wife of the deceased, to give vent to the grief that gripped her heart. "Diblaim, I crave your love and you starve me with your absence. I know I will dream in the night that you are still with me, then awaken to discover you are gone forever." She rent the edge of her sackcloth and beat her fists on her chest. To the left of Salome her eleven-year-old daughter sighed in torment at her mother's song; oblivious to his sister's chagrin, Salome's seventeen-year-old son gripped her elbow and tried to comfort her.

But Salome was inconsolable. "Oh, my husband, with curls as black as night and tender lamb's eyes, how shall I give you up? How you refreshed me in life, but there is no consolation in your death. How much better to have died myself than to suffer the agony of your death, my beloved, my Diblaim."

The next morning Gomer carefully watched her mother, afraid she might have truly awakened surprised by her father's death; but she seemed more intent on receiving hordes of villagers into their tent carrying provisions in their hands and consolations on their lips.

Nabin, a local priest, bent to Salome's daughter and whispered, "You must be strong, Gomer. Your mother needs you more than ever now that your father is dead." He spoke in a raspy whisper.

Must you voice his death? Gomer's thoughts reeled. One moment her father had been laughing with her, dubbing her the "apple of his eye," and the next he was gone.

The strange old woman at the edge of the woods said a demon had squeezed his heart till it burst. A shudder convulsed Gomer.

She watched with eyes that took in more than her eleven years should as the pompous priest stepped closer than was necessary to her still attractive mother, Salome. The Widow Salome, everyone now called her. Gomer looked up at the priest. Nabin looked so wise in his jeweled ephod and cap. Perhaps he had some answers about her father's death.

"Diblaim was an honorable man, a most beloved man, and highly respected among the elders," Nabin intoned. "His wisdom will be sorely missed at the city gates."

Oh, Abba, how will I fare without you? Gomer agonized with a moan. She could not trust her voice, so she spoke her grief with a more silent ceremony than the rest of the mourners.

"No, we shall not soon forget our friend, Diblaim." The priest unhooked his thumbs from his sparkling ephod and took Salome's arm. He patted her hand and smiled sympathetically; but to Gomer his lips curved grotesquely and his lowered voice sounded more like a hiss than a whisper.

Nabin supported the weeping widow with an embrace. "The people of the village have given sheep and goats for you, and the elders gathered alms of silver and gold to assuage your family's grief."

Salome nodded her appreciation, blinking innocently at the priest through tear-clouded eyes. Nabin leaned down to Gomer and touched her chin with a heroic air. "Do not fear for your father, child. He fares better than we. The God of Abraham has taken him to his reward."

"The Lord God took my father?" Gomer breathed incredulously.

"Why yes, child," Nabin's eyes glazed mystically.

"Someday He will gather together all his people with Him."

"So the Lord God of Israel is to blame for this!" Gomer exploded. "I thought you said He loves us. What kind of love leaves a family alone to starve and grieve for a father?"

"Gomer!" Salome admonished. Her eyes were red with weeping, but she stopped dabbing at them and glared at her daughter.

"What does serving your cruel God mean? That we will be rewarded with death, with losing the ones we love?" Gomer was wide-eyed, trying to stop the tears that threatened to flood her face. But no one answered her. The mourners only gaped in stunned silence at her unexpected outburst. "If this is true, if God is the one who took my father, then Father was as deceived by Him as you are. But *I* will not be the Lord's victim."

The priest slapped Gomer. "Blasphemy! You will have respect for the name of the Lord God. If your father heard your words he would set you before the city gates to be judged by the elders."

"No, he wouldn't. Not Abba!" Gomer bit her lip and searched for a comforting glance among the mass of villagers. Finding none, she shoved through the crowd and fought her way to the tent's flap, screaming back at them, "I hate your God!" Gomer heard her mother pleading, "No, let her go. She hasn't yet learned to fear the Lord."

Blinded by tears, Gomer pushed past the last of the curious crowd. Her retreat left a wake of chalky dust as bleating sheep and goats scampered from before her, trampling the lavender flowers scattered over the dry terrain. The voice of the cursing shepherd followed her.

She strove from the path past boulders and scrubby

bushes. The last clay house in the village seemed to spy her every movement. Shuddering, Gomer determined to hide herself in the elusive rock partridge's domain.

Engrossed in leaving Beth-el behind, she forced herself forward on the slippery, lush grass carpet of the hillside. Only gradually did she slow her pace, to find that she was choking down mouthfuls of turbulent, ash-like earth. She closed her mouth, but still the gritty dryness spread into her throat. Finally certain she was alone, Gomer found the hillslope that she was looking for: *her* hill, dotted with patches of yellow daisies.

She staggered to the summit and threw herself face down on the ground. "Where is justice? Who will stand as witness against You?" she screamed, and pounded the unrelenting earth. "I loved him, and You took him away. Don't You care about me? I *need* Abba."

Silence was the only response. *He doesn't care enough to even answer*, Gomer thought bitterly. Anger exploded within her. In threatening tones she addressed the cruel God she knew as the Lord God of Israel. "I vow to hurt You as You have hurt me. I don't know just how, but I will find a way to flee this village. My life will stand as witness against what You've done to me." Cradling her head in her arms, she wept bitterly until she thought she could never cry again. Exhausted, Gomer lay still. The bitterness drained momentarily, but it left a galling emptiness that was much more painful.

She rolled upon her back and dried her face with the sleeve of her tunic. She blinked at the solace of the bright, blue sky. The serenity seemed to make her problems fade as smoothly as the wind-scattered patches of clouds drifting high overhead.

"Abba?" Even before she whispered his name she knew it would make her sad. She was about to cry again

13

when a puff of wind blew her hair back. It felt like a caress—but then it passed on. She sensed a presence.

"Abba?" she asked with diminishing anguish. Her wonder increased. The wind remained calm. She felt foolish. "I should know better." Gomer sat up and swept the dirt from her arms. "A God like the Lord would never let my father return to me," she snorted.

A gentle breeze swept over her and seemed to call her to peace. Gomer trembled. *It is not my father but the Lord!* She stood and faced heaven in defiance. "You dare to call me to peace after You tore my life apart?" she shouted at the sky. "You give only the peace found in death. Find some other fool to trick with Your false serenity. I desire life and the love I had from my father. And I will find that love You stole from me, somehow, someday. Leave me, I want nothing to do with You!"

Suddenly the gentle wind stilled and Gomer succumbed to the refreshment of a more alluring breeze. Though it gently stirred her skirts, this subtle wind, soliciting her thoughts and desires, was as different from the first as evening from dawn. A hunger for fulfillment was born within her as the wind courted her with its hypnotic touch.

She closed her eyes and tried to imagine one, unlike the Lord, who knew how to love, satisfying her desires forever. Her imagination soared with the windswept clouds. They seemed to form a ruggedly handsome face in the heavens. The slight breeze played with the ends of her hair and tickled her face. Gomer giggled.

1

Israel is chasing the wind, yes, shepherding a whirlwind—a dangerous game!

Hosea 12:1

Hidden in the shadow of her mother's tent, Gomer withdrew a brightly colored scarf from the folds of her tunic. Her black eyes sparkled. Though guilt over neglected chores pricked her adolescent conscience, she forbade it to intrude on a few moments of imagined pleasure.

Gomer closed her eyes to conjure up the familiar image. She slowly drew the scarf over her forearm, as though it were the touch of another. She basked in the coolness captured by the silky material before the midmorning sun could chase it away. Draping the scarlet prize through her fingers, she caressed her velvet cheek, casting a fiery glow on her exotic features. Holding her head askance, her shoulder-length hair formed black ringlets over the crimson scarf, as she dreamed of the one for whom her soul longed.

Enchanted by an inflamed desire to meet with him in

reality, Gomer began to sway rhythmically, imitating movements she had learned from the marketplace dancers. She swirled the seemingly weightless scarf over her head several times before her brother Dan's voice within the tent brought her arms, and her daydreams, to an abrupt halt.

"Mother, I'm glad I found you alone. I must speak to you about what happened at the marketplace. I wanted to tell you last night, but you were already asleep when we returned."

Gomer listened as her widowed mother, Salome, replied, "My son, I am so weary of spinning these drab animal hairs. Is there not a way our sheep could provide me with colored wool?"

Gomer heard the bristly sound of wool being pulled from beneath her mother's arm and knew she continued twisting the web absently as she spoke.

"Perhaps scarlet. Ah, yes, scarlet would be nice. Of a truth, anything but the tiresome black and white would do."

"Mother," Dan interrupted her chatter. "Please listen, I need to speak with you."

"I think I would like blue wool too. The color of the Great Sea," Salome prattled on.

Usually Dan allowed his mother's habitual avalanche of thoughts to run its course, but by his sigh Gomer knew he was impatient.

"Mother, how would you like for Gomer to be married?"

Gomer cringed. *Oh, let it not be that middle-aged villager with the vineyard. He always smells of vinegar.*

"Married?" Salome laughed. "Gomer isn't ready for marriage. True, she *is* thirteen summers, but she can't even cook and can sew only well enough to hold two cloths together. The artistry of her fingers goes no further than that, though it is through no fault of my own. The Lord knows I've tried to teach her."

"You may change your mind about her readiness when you hear what I have to say." Dan paused.

"Well, do go on," urged Salome. "We haven't all day to spend talking. From the limp feel of this wool I fear our sheep to be unhealthy. This is no time to be idle if you are to restore them to health. But praise be to the Lord for the late rains this year. Its abundance shows in the greenness of the hillsides, and the rich pasture will surely strengthen our sheep. Have you noticed how—"

Dan stamped his foot. "Will you hear me or not?"

"Now you behave as Gomer," Salome admonished with a chuckle. Gomer giggled at the comment.

"Mother!" Dan raised his voice. "The *high priest* wishes Gomer for his wife!"

Gomer suddenly felt nauseated. *Having a priest for a husband would be like being married to my mother!*

Salome's voice squeaked with excitement. "The high priest wants *my* daughter in marriage?"

"Yes," Dan said. "At least I pray he still does."

"What do you mean?" Salome said anxiously.

"It is all so unbelievable, Mother. Yesterday, while we were shopping in the marketplace, Gomer ran ahead pretending to look at the fabric and such, but I knew she was heading for the dancing girls again. I would have followed, as you instructed, but a dark stranger approached me. So steady were his eyes, and so noble his air, that at first I thought him to be a foreign prince. Then I saw by his clothing that he was just a distinguished servant of high rank. When he greeted me in the name of his master, Amaziah, the chief priest of the king's chapel in Beth-el, my heart fainted in fear."

"There is no reason it should," his mother said. "You have lived a righteous life. And no husband could have cared for me better. You are truly the reward of my old age." Salome's voice softened.

Dan ignored his mother's praise. "Then the servant begged me to accept *these* as tokens of Amaziah's sincerity." A jingling sound came from inside the tent, and Gomer heard her mother gasp.

"After he disclosed the high priest's request, the servant pointed to an upper window of the king's chapel. Though the temple was some distance away I could see his master, Amaziah, nod in greeting."

"And he wanted *our* Gomer for his bride?" Salome repeated blankly.

"Listen to me, Mother," Dan said. "I have not told you how Gomer may have forfeited everything. When the servant left, I sought Gomer to tell her of her good fortune. But the words churned like gall when I found her with those same dancing girls. She was mimicking their movements right in the midst of the marketplace, as if she were one of them! I am glad you were not there to see the crowd of unseemly men that had gathered round her."

"Did the high priest see her with those harlots?" Salome asked weakly.

"I quickly looked back at the window to find out, but Amaziah was gone and his servant had disappeared too. I cannot be certain, Mother, but if the priest saw Gomer's behavior, I fear he'll withdraw his proposal. My heart sank as Gomer ran up to me proudly displaying a few coins the crowd had thrown at her!"

Even through the thick goat-hair walls of the tent Gomer could hear the sound of slow thumping. She knew it was her mother beating her chest mournfully, as she often did in despair over her daughter's actions.

Oh, I see, Gomer thought indignantly. *It's all right for Dan to accept payment on my behalf, but I cannot.* She saw no wrong in the natural beauty of a dance or why dancing would cast doubt on one's virtue.

Words seemed to form in the breeze. *Come to me, Gomer,* came the familiar call of the one her soul had been seeking. *Let go of your grief and I will comfort you.*

Gomer looked longingly at the top of a knoll where the wind blew free. *I knew you would call, my love.* She dropped the scarf, as though everything she held dear was unimportant compared to that which called to her on the hill. She barely remembered running through the field and climbing the embankment. All her thoughts were enveloped in her fantasy.

Gomer waited on the top of the hill. As the wind framed her maturing form, she closed her eyes and meditated on him whom she loved. An unfettered wind coaxed her to feel like the goddess Anath, queen of heaven. She imagined the breeze that combed her raven-black hair was her mythic lover running his fingers through it. *No one is like you.* She lifted her face into the sky for the phantom kiss, then brushed her lips reverently at the imagined touch.

The image faded suddenly when Gomer noticed that her soiled hand left a smear across her mouth. It was a disgusting reminder of how she really lived. The effort to rub the blemish off puckered her mouth into a childish pout. *Some goddess I am,* she thought in disillusionment. *Perhaps I should accept the priest's offer. At least I could escape this life that has kept me so long a prisoner. Then I would be free to answer when HE calls again on the wind!*

Her thoughts were diverted by the unexpected sounds of an approaching caravan, shattering what remained of her fantasy. Still, she was pleased that it was passing ear-

19

lier than usual. She loved to sit at the top of the knoll and dream of traveling with the train to faraway places. As she scanned the road below, the dust that stung her eyes and the smell that filled her nostrils told her this was not the merchants' caravan she was expecting.

What should have been a caravan master was a large Ethiopian servant perched on the lead donkey. Almost kingly in appearance, his darkened skin contrasted handsomely against his bright vest and glittering scabbard. Following on foot were three maidservants leading a camel harnessed in glittering leather and draped with a brightly striped blanket fringed with tinkling bells. An unoccupied, ornate saddle topped the camel's hump, as though waiting for an honored personage. Tethered behind were two more camels that looked naked by comparison. An ass, burdened with bulging packs, surrounded by a dozen sheep and goats, brought up the rear. Three menservants' shouts grew audible as they wove among the animals, keeping them in line.

At the sound of falling pebbles, the dark servant turned suddenly to see Gomer scramble down the side of the hill toward him. He lifted his arm.

"Ho!" He shouted a halt to his company in a booming voice, then smiled broadly at Gomer. His huge white teeth glowed. "Greetings, Gomer, honored sister of Dan, the son of Diblaim."

"How do you know me, sir?" Gomer said, stunned by his familiarity. The answer was evident when she noted that the unusual caravan consisted of only servants. "I see the high priest has sent you."

The head servant threw his head back in a laugh that was slightly condescending, yet seemed filled with friendly warmth.

"You perceive well, little one. I am Ka'Tan. I have

come in the name of my master Amaziah who has sent these gifts to your family, hoping to gain their favor." With a sweep of his arm he included the entire caravan.

"Is this all he thinks I'm worth?" Gomer teased. She assumed the bold stance of a soldier returning victorious from battle and laughed.

The older man's eyes sparkled as he let himself be carried along in the camaraderie. "Count yourself blessed, young one. As Amaziah's desire for your hand increased, so did his generosity."

"Since I've never met Amaziah, may I ask what has caused this desire?" Gomer asked, puzzled.

"My master is a connoisseur of the dance." Ka'Tan winked.

Gomer laughed deeply, remembering the slow thumping of her mother's despair. *You needn't have worried, Mother,* she thought. *It seems the servant of your God, at least, has an appreciation for artistry.*

The restless scuffling of the animals' feet brought Gomer's eyes back to meet the amiable gaze of Ka'Tan. "May I escort you to the tent of my mother?"

"Please," Ka'Tan gestured to the unoccupied camel. "Would you like to ride with us?"

In childish exuberance Gomer did not bother to answer but began circling the beast, excitedly searching for a place to mount. Once astride she found the comfort surprising. In a beast so lacking in beauty Gomer hadn't expected anything pleasurable.

With Gomer leading, they rounded the knoll and were in sight of her home. From her exalted position it looked as small and insignificant as she had always thought it to be. Gomer was eager to look down on the faces of her mother and Dan. She hadn't long to wait as the tinkling of the camels' bells brought them out of the tent in curiosity. The gray hair of her mother contrasted with the dark tousled hair of her brother in the daylight.

Salome clasped her heart in shock at seeing Gomer upon the richly garbed animal. Dan squinted and shaded his eyes as though unable to believe what he was seeing. Neither seemed able to speak until the caravan had stopped before them.

"Oh, Mother," Gomer giggled, "if you could only see your face."

Her mother answered in rebuke. "What mischief have you wrought now, my daughter?"

Touching Salome's arm, Dan whispered, "Mother, this is the servant that I spoke to you about."

She turned a crimson face to the servant and begged, "Please forgive my rudeness. You are most welcome in our dwelling."

"Many thanks." Ka'Tan bowed his head, barely hiding his amusement. "I am Ka'Tan, head servant of Amaziah, the high priest of the king's chapel in Beth-el. Amaziah sends his humble greetings and blesses your home with peace and prosperity. He implores you to accept these few gifts in return for your favor." He again gestured toward the caravan.

Mother and son staggered at the assembled wealth. They were clearly captivated.

Clearing his throat, Ka'Tan asked, "May I speak to you within?"

Embarrassed once more at her lack of hospitality, Salome bowed low as Ka'Tan dismounted. "My lord, the small comforts of our home are yours. Please partake freely."

Ka'Tan commanded the servants to unload as Dan and his mother exchanged a smile behind him. Before following the men into the tent Salome hurried over to

Gomer, who was parading her camel around the grounds.

"Where is your head, child?" she hissed. "Get down and see to the refreshment of our guest." She bustled into the tent, not waiting to hear Gomer's agitated sigh.

Having served them, Gomer resumed her place behind the tent to dream about the life that lay ahead at Beth-el. The thoughts that occupied her mind were not of Amaziah or marriage, but of leaving her mother's tent forever. *I will do whatever I please whenever I please*, she promised herself. *Even dance!* She sighed contentedly, recalling the spectrum of color flashing and swirling in the marketplace as she danced. She stood and twirled around, imagining herself robed with such colors.

On the last swirl she glimpsed her mother staring wistfully at her. "Oh, Mother, I didn't see you there."

Ignoring her daughter's words, Salome walked briskly to a grassy mound and situated herself upon it. She motioned for Gomer to sit beside her. Gomer sat, certain she would be reprimanded for her performance. Instead, she was startled when her mother reached clumsily for her hand. Gomer felt awkward.

"The Lord has smiled on us, Gomer." Salome patted her daughter's hand. "Amaziah, the priest at Beth-el, desires you for his wife. I would like to know what you think on this matter."

"Will I live in Beth-el?"

"Yes, within the king's chapel."

"Then I will go."

"With no more reason than that? Child, is that all you care about?" Gomer's mother withdrew her hand. "I should have known that your consent would have little to do with *marriage*. Have you really given any consideration to your betrothed, or are you only concerned whether you will be near the marketplace so you can dance with the harlots?"

"Does dancing make you a harlot?" Without waiting for a reply, Gomer spat, "I'll tell you what dancing has made *me*: the wife of the high priest!"

"How dare you speak such abominations in the same breath with the name of God's chosen!" Her mother clasped her hands in the air, looked heavenward and beseeched, "Lord God, have mercy upon the foolishness of her youth!"

Gomer pulled Salome's clasped hands down in order to look her squarely in the face, then spoke as if Salome were the child.

"Mother, Ka'Tan has told me that if Amaziah had not seen me dancing, the packs upon the ass would not have bulged so generously. You and Dan are foolish to think that a 'man of God' is above reproach. You say the Lord has smiled on us. I say it was not the desire of *God*, but of Amaziah." Gomer raised her eyebrows precociously.

Salome was throwing a handful of dirt on her head in the agony of her daughter's blasphemous words when Dan's voice interrupted with a piercing whisper.

"Mother! Gomer! Hold your peace. Ka'Tan can hear your every word! He wishes to hear Gomer's reply, not your biting tongues. Would you have him think we are a family of jackals?"

"Tell Ka'Tan I am ready now," Gomer said to Dan, but her eyes never left her mother's face.

Salome jumped to her feet. She dusted and straightened her tunic, nervously aware of Gomer's intense stare. As though making a final attempt to exert her authority, Salome said, "At least present yourself properly to our guest." She shook the dirt from her head cloth and roughly placed it on Gomer's head, then turned to march triumphantly into the tent. Gomer followed, not knowing whether to be shocked or furious. Dan walked behind, shaking his head at them.

Ka'Tan stood as Gomer entered the tent. "Have you given your consent, my lady?"

"I would be most honored." Gomer almost bowed.

"Excellent," Ka'Tan smiled. "Shall we see if the dowry meets with your approval, master Dan?"

Mother and daughter were left alone to make final preparations for the journey. The painful silence became a dividing wall between them. Salome avoided Gomer's gaze and tried to busy herself. She opened a chest that held all the family's belongings and was slowly packing Gomer's tunics and undergarments when Gomer stopped her.

"I don't think I'll need those. I'm not marrying a shepherd, Mother, but the chief priest of the royal chapel."

Salome said nothing but closed the chest quietly. Crossing the tent, she picked up a greasy cloth that held some cakes left over from the morning meal. She looked at her daughter with a question in her eyes.

Seeing the bread her mother held, Gomer shook her head and laughed. "Amaziah's generosity seems to have robbed us of the pretense of busyness."

Salome managed a small chuckle. In the silence that followed the two women stared at the ground. Salome turned her gaze toward the tent flap blowing in the breeze.

"Gomer, when your father named you, I reminded him I had birthed a daughter, not a son. Of course, he knew you were a girl and laughed when I suggested that he didn't. He wanted to know what was wrong with giving *his* daughter a man's name. He always wanted a boy first, then a girl, so your birth 'completed' his desire for our family. That's why he named you Gomer—one who completes."

Interrupting her reverie, Salome turned her full attention to Gomer. "It pains my heart that he cannot see you now that you are honoring *his* name by becoming the wife of the high priest. I wish he were here now so he could say all the words that I cannot." She bowed her head, covering her face with her hands.

Gomer laid a still hand on her mother's head. There were no loving strokes to Gomer's touch, but a certain comfort. It had been a long time since she felt anything but irritation toward her mother. "Tell me more about him, Mamma," she asked softly.

"Mamma?" Salome looked gratefully into Gomer's eyes. "You haven't called me Mamma since you were a small child." She smiled, then looked away again.

"Oh, Gomer, your father was most manly. He stood a head above all men. Not only in stature, but in virtue. I don't remember ever seeing him unhappy either. But he was not frivolous," Salome quickly defined. "He was devoted to the Lord God and honored by men." She paused and looked meaningfully at Gomer.

With a sigh Gomer rolled her eyes. "*Do* go on, Mother."

"I remember once during our betrothal," Salome laughed to herself, "he was sitting among the elders in the gates near the marketplace (his counsel was highly esteemed), when he called me away from my father's fig stand.

"When I came to him he said, 'Your wisdom is precious to me, my love; you were even named for the wisdom of Solomon. The elders and I have need of such a gift.' Well, as you can imagine, I could not fathom his meaning. And the elders' faces held looks that made me feel not wholly welcome." Salome raised her eyebrows.

"He proceeded to tell me that they had philosophized all morning over what to do with a certain large sum of money that had been collected from the offerings. It seemed they suspected the money had been given from ill-gotten gain. And your father wanted to know how *I* would solve the issue! Well, I had never heard of such a thing as asking a woman to advise the elders. But, then, that was your father."

Gomer was enjoying the idea of her straightlaced mother as an accomplice to such an improper act. "So, what did you advise?" she urged her to continue.

Salome was delighted by Gomer's sudden attention. She scrunched her shoulders up about her neck girlishly and said, "Well, I simply gave them the wisdom of the common people. I said, 'I know not if the money paid me for my figs comes from the hand of a blasphemer or an angel. Should I then not give it with a pure heart to the Lord?'

"Those elders for once had no words, although I could tell what they were thinking. But, when your father said to them, 'As God gave Deborah to Israel, so He has given my betrothed to me,' I knew their thoughts would never be voiced!"

Mother and daughter laughed loudly together, but the moment was bittersweet. Reaching to pat her daughter's hand, Salome said, "I pray that the Lord God of Israel grant you a marriage such as your father and I had."

When Gomer turned away and said nothing, Salome voiced concern. "Daughter, do you understand that by being given in marriage you are to share a man's bed?"

"I understand that I am to be a wife, but as for his bed, isn't that only to be understood by experience?"

"Well, yes, but it is understood well in some marriages, and not so well in others."

"Was it well in yours, Mother?"

Salome's eyes twinkled. "Ah, very well."

"Then it will surely be well with mine," Gomer said in a matter-of-fact tone.

The twinkle faded from Salome's eyes as her face became agitated. "When my mother spoke with me about marriage, she said rightly, 'It is upon your husband's bed that you pave the way in which you will walk.' Gomer," Salome said, "the stones with which you pave your path must be hewn with honor."

Dan stuck his head in the opening of the tent. "If it is convenient, Ka'Tan wishes to present the gifts now."

"In a moment. We are not finished," Salome replied.

"Yes, we are," Gomer said quickly.

Salome looked pained, but she shrugged her shoulders in resignation. "So be it."

As they came out of the tent, Ka'Tan positioned himself before them. Bowing low he said, "My master Amaziah, the high priest of the king's chapel in Beth-el, hopes these meager offerings will in some small way atone for the treasure he is receiving from the bosom of your family."

A manservant immediately stepped forward, both forearms hung with gold, silver, and ivory trinkets. He deposited them in a glittering bundle at the feet of Salome. The pile grew with a seemingly endless flow of precious jewels, fragrant spices, ointments, materials made from fine twisted linen, magnificently detailed pottery, and urns filled with olive oil and perfumes.

As a finishing touch, two menservants displayed themselves before Dan, and two maidservants before his mother. Ka'Tan bowed slightly. "Master Dan will need shepherds for his growing flocks, and Mistress will need additional help to replace the loss of her only daughter."

Ka'Tan's words brought forth an audible gasp from

Salome. Her fist involuntarily flew to her chest and she glared at Ka'Tan as if he were a thief. When Gomer's fingers enveloped her mother's fist, still tightly pressed against her heart, Salome looked suddenly near hysteria.

Brusquely clasping Gomer's face in her hands, Salome burst forth in a flood of emotion. "Gomer, why is this moment filled with terror? This should be a time of rejoicing. Why does my heart deceive me?"

Dan pulled Salome to him. "Your heart speaks for the protective instinct you have. It is the mark of a godly mother. Is this not the result of your prayers that have risen up to the Lord God for these many years?"

Gomer nodded, fearful that her mother might yet destroy this chance at a new life.

"Yes. Yes, but . . ." Salome confided to her son. "Gomer is but a child. I fear that my instructions have been inadequate. I must speak with her more."

"Mother," Dan prodded gently, "if she has not heeded your wisdom all her childhood, a few minutes more will not result in sudden maturity. You know Gomer will always see to her own survival. Besides, there is no more time. They must depart quickly if they are to return in safety before nightfall."

"As the Lord God lives," Ka'Tan swore, as he produced a chain bearing the signet ring of his master, "I swear by the seal of Amaziah, chief priest of the king's chapel at Beth-el, I myself shall perish ere I allow danger to dare draw nigh unto Gomer, the treasured daughter of Diblaim."

Gomer's mother kissed Amaziah's ring in appreciation. "As the Lord God lives," she breathed, sealing the oath. Still fear remained on her face. She watched dumbfounded as a servant assisted Gomer's mounting of the royally draped beast.

In a silent salutation, Gomer slid her mother's veil from her head. Bending low, she handed it to Salome with a bewitching smile. "It itches," she said simply.

As the slow plodding gait of the camels took Gomer away, she looked back at her mother disappearing from view. She was sorry she did. It seemed the fist that habitually flew to her mother's chest and the painful look in her mother's eyes would be imprinted forever as a blemished memory.

She would not miss much about her family. Her daydreams had prepared her for only the best life had to offer. If the farewells had lingered any longer the bitterness Gomer felt toward her mother would have surfaced. Depriving her of her dreams was unforgivable. Gomer shook her head in fury at the thought. *Even now my mother tries to alter my life.*

For diversion Gomer spurred her camel alongside Ka'-Tan's. Mimicking his authorative airs, she said, "Hail, Ka'Tan, head servant of Amaziah, chief priest of the king's chapel at Beth-el." The corners of her mouth quivered in merriment. "Tell, what heroics do you propose if 'danger dares to draw nigh me'?"

Ka'Tan winked at the manservant walking at his side and joined in the teasing. "Ah, my lady," he rolled his eyes heavenward. "If danger takes form as a ravenous bear that desires to dine upon your sweet flesh, then I would tear asunder my arm from its socket, and beg it to drink of the marrow of my bones instead.

"And if threat comes by way of the fierce lioness lying in wait to shred your features into an unrecognizable mass, then I would rip out my tongue and offer the dripping sacrifice in appeasement, while you escape unharmed. And if we stumble into the ambush of a band of marauding thieves, and they desire to—"

"Hold your tongue *there*, Ka'Tan, or by the use of your own blade I will hold it myself!" Gomer laughed, her face pale.

"Does my lady think me insincere?" Ka'Tan asked, his eyes widened in feigned innocence. "If I speak not truthfully may the gods strike me with leprosy, palsy, and bloody boils that never cease oozing the yellow sap of sickness and disease."

As her stomach grew queasy, Gomer laid one arm across her midsection, and with the other reached in jest for where she knew Ka'Tan's blade would be sheathed within his cloak. "I gave warning," she squealed.

The servant walking beside Ka'Tan exploded in laughter. To Gomer, Ka'Tan had more than proved himself to be valuable in diversions. She was finally free!

Gomer drew her lips in an upside-down grin in a vain effort to suppress the laugh she knew was coming. She threw her head back and closed her eyes tightly, but the attempt was futile. Her hair bounced as her head bobbed in uncontrollable throaty laughter, reaching voluminous peaks, subsiding into a fatigued but satisfied sigh. Wiping the tears from her tightly shut eyes, she opened first one eye and then the other, wary of the conspicuous silence surrounding her.

Three pairs of eyes stared in surprise. Her bold laughter was more characteristic of a young man having finished a flagon of wine, than a meek young girl betrothed to the high priest.

"Since our acquaintance will be long," Ka'Tan chided, "I *pray* that your laugh will improve with age, my lady."

2

They are all adulterers; as a baker's oven is constantly aflame—except while he kneads the dough and waits for it to rise—so are these people constantly aflame with lust.
Stay away from her, for she is wedded to idolatry.

Hosea 7:4; 4:17

The voice of Amaziah's forerunner bellowed above the usual excessive noise of the merchants at day's end.

"Make way for the honorable Gomer, betrothed of Amaziah," the forerunner shouted, clearing a path by prodding with his rod the slow to respond and the ever-present lazy dogs of the street. They growled threateningly at the interruption of their daily meal of garbage thrown from the windows by the women of Beth-el.

The confining streets were lined with people who stared at Gomer in curiosity. *Let them stare,* she thought, straightening her shoulders with pride. *After all, I am the honorable Gomer!* The dust of the journey and the simple shepherd's clothing could not dispel her air of mastery.

The caravan turned onto a street that encompassed the chapel. Gomer's sophistication fled. "We're here!" she squealed to Ka'Tan with the childish delight of a suckling at the feast of his weaning.

In all the times she made the journey with Dan to the marketplace, Gomer had never paid much heed to the elegant temple, but this time it held her undivided attention. It was to be her home. She could tell the walls had recently been scrubbed down with limestone. She wondered if it had been done for her arrival. They shone like a pearl in the lengthening rays of sunlight and seemed to sparkle just for her.

Gomer caught a glimpse of movement on the rooftop. When she squinted her eyes against the glare of the sun, she could see an aging man lean his weighty frame against a low parapet. His eyes seemed to rake the crowded street like a vulture searching for prey. At almost the same time Gomer saw him, his eyes rested on her.

He clapped sharply and a servant appeared. With a sinking feeling in her stomach Gomer hoped that this was not the high priest.

Once inside the gate of the chapel the company dismounted. The forerunner led their camels through the outer courtyard to the stables.

"By your leave, my lady," Ka'Tan turned to Gomer and bowed. "Reumah will escort you to the baths, that you may refresh yourself, while I report to our master, Amaziah."

"*Our* master?" Gomer raised her eyebrows.

Ka'Tan ignored her comment and crisply walked away.

He certainly has become somber, Gomer thought, but the rich beauty surrounding her quickly absorbed all her attention. She drank it in as she followed Reumah. *This is to be my home!*

The floor of the outer courtyard, where they had dismounted, was of hewn stone so highly polished that it looked like marble. As they neared the south end of the yard, the scent of orange blossoms and fragrant aloes intoxicated her. She followed the scent with her eyes and saw that orange and aloe trees surrounded a quartzite fountain, which lent a merry sound to the lonely court.

They passed quickly into a tiled corridor that caused even their soft leather sandals to click. The servants lighting the lamps along the corridor seemed oblivious to the presence of the women, although Gomer suspected the news of her arrival had preceded her.

At the end of the passageway they stopped at an arched door of cedar encircled with a deeply carved pattern of grapevines. Reumah unlocked the door and stepped back for Gomer to enter.

Quickly growing accustomed to being honored in this way, Gomer entered the door regally; but she was not prepared for what she saw.

A woman stepped forward and bowed. "I am Hodesh. I have been assigned as your handmaiden. Our lord, Amaziah, offers you the refreshment of perfumed waters, my lady. He hopes you will be pleased."

A startled Gomer had not yet glanced at the woman Hodesh. Her eyes were still locked upon a half dozen men stationed around the pool, fanning the air with palm branches. "Am I expected to disrobe in the presence of these men?" Gomer demanded.

"Truly, mistress, these men have been blind from birth," Hodesh hastened to assure her, as she held out her arms to receive Gomer's soiled garments.

Still wary, Gomer stood partially hidden behind Hodesh, eyeing the eunuchs suspiciously as she undressed. Her suspicion resurfaced when she stepped noiselessly toward the sunken pool and the nearest man held out a large sponge directly in front of her.

Stepping back, she said sharply, "I thought you said they could not see!"

Hodesh quickly reassured her. "My lady, the years without sight have sharpened their other senses tremendously. They are able to hear what we cannot and to discern what goes on about them."

Reluctantly Gomer eased into the scented bath. The swirling water soon relieved her of doubts concerning anything. Nothing mattered save the tranquility that carried her away on rolls of aromatic waves. Gomer had not dreamed that such a soothing experience existed. The cool bath refreshed her. The sight of the smooth, hard marble continuing across the floor and up the pillars to tower over the eunuchs, proclaimed that her daydreams had indeed become reality.

If only you were here my happiness would be complete. Gomer thought dreamily of her illusory lover.

She closed her eyes to meet with him in her dreams once more while Hodesh urged her head gently back to rest upon the rounded pool edge. The handmaiden filled a vase with water and trickled it through Gomer's hair, as she expertly massaged away the dust and sand. Gomer felt as if this were the reality she were born to. Her prior existence was but a dream.

Too soon Hodesh hurried her out of the bath and quickly anointed and robed her. Gomer was deposited in the doorway of the high priest's sleeping quarters while her handmaiden entered the adjoining room where Amaziah sat waiting. She saw Hodesh quickly prostrate herself before him, awaiting permission to present Gomer.

Amaziah was leaning back against the wall, propping himself up with the plush cushions. His crossed legs would hardly stay in position, for the thick folds of his belly kept pushing them away.

Before him a low table, crafted of wood and overlaid with gold, held a tempting array of fruit. The walls of the room were made of carved cedar inlaid with precariously placed plaques of ivory. They reflected their owner's delight in beauty. The light and spicy aroma that permeated the room came from two candlesticks burning perfumed oil. Gomer recognized the scent as cinnamon.

Amaziah clapped his hands twice. In response Hodesh rose. "Sir, I most heartily present to you, chief priest of Israel, the lovely Gomer, daughter of Diblaim."

"Well, do send her in." He was careful not to look at Gomer until she had been presented.

Hodesh backed from the room to Gomer's side.

"What shall I say to a high priest?" Gomer hissed, suddenly afraid.

"Oh, my lady, do not fear. Your appearance will speak for you. But your beauty is so great, do not be surprised if the master is speechless."

"Come, come!" Amaziah spoke sharply.

The confidence of Hodesh and the truth of her words gave Gomer the assurance she needed to walk forward, holding her head high.

She eyed Amaziah cautiously. Gomer did not know what she had been expecting, but this same weighty, aging man she had seen on the roof was unacceptable. How could she bow to *him* as the substitute for the lover she had always dreamed of?

She studied him closer and saw strong desire burn within his eyes. With smugness Gomer thought, *So a priest is no different than other men. If I can keep him in hand, then being the wife of the high priest may be tolerable.* Though he was no joy to behold, his wealth and

36

rank were enough to make up for his grotesque appearance. She weighed the advantages and smiled at him.

Amaziah rose as quickly as his oversized frame would allow. Stretching out his hand toward her apparel he said, "Are you pleased with the dress?"

"Oh, yes, my lord. It is very pleasant." Gomer carefully crossed her arms and ran her fingertips up her shoulders. Hugging herself she said, "The fabric feels like silk next to my skin. Here, feel for yourself." Letting go of her shoulders she held out a corner of her sleeve for inspection.

Gladly accepting the fabric between his fingers and her gaze within his, Amaziah smiled. "Yes, exquisite, exquisite."

Gomer found his reaction to her teasing satisfying. "And look," she went on, "how the dress seems to dance." She stretched her dress out to arm's length and gracefully twirled before him, allowing the cloth to ripple in billowing waves, confident that it reminded him of the dance he had seen her do in the marketplace.

Amaziah looked more than a little uncomfortable. Quickly changing the subject, he said, "Gomer, may we speak on the matter of our forthcoming marriage?"

Gomer reluctantly stopped. Without waiting for a reply, Amaziah clapped his hands. Immediately a manservant appeared through the door from his bedchambers. He ordered the man to fluff the pillows on the floor for Gomer and to offer her some fruit.

"Please, Gomer, comfort yourself," a more composed Amaziah gestured toward the cushions. "At the first watch of the morning I am sending twenty servants with invitations to our wedding. One will, of course, be sent to your mother and brother. Other invitations will be sent to various officials." Leaning toward her he said with emphasis, "And a party of servants will leave for Samaria to request the presence of Jeroboam at our wedding."

"The king?"

"To be sure. The king seldom misses our feasts. It is well known among the friends of the king that he takes much pleasure in celebrations. Why, once he gave a five-day feast because he had an unusually pleasant dream!"

Gomer was not impressed by Amaziah's familiarity with the king. Nothing about the high priest was impressive, but she smiled at him anyway.

"But enough of this for now. I'm sure you are tired. I have given Hodesh as your handmaiden. She will see you to the private bridal chambers and instruct you in all that you will need to know about living in the king's chapel." Amaziah reached out to touch Gomer's cheek. "The wait until our wedding feast will be painfully slow for me."

Gomer lowered her eyelids.

Hodesh proved to be a very good instructor. Too good. She kept the three days prior to the wedding a whirlwind of tours, bathings, and anointings, with so many instructions that Gomer gave up listening.

None of Hodesh's detailed instructions mattered to Gomer until the third day, when they observed a roomful of women making perfumed oils. Gomer turned to Hodesh. "Does it always take so many servants?"

"Servants?" Hodesh repeated blankly, glancing into the room. "Do you not know?"

"Know what?"

"Oh," mumbled Hodesh, "I thought everyone understood how to prepare ointments . . ."

Gomer knew by her response that Hodesh was hiding

something. She determined to find out what, as soon as she was settled into married life.

At dawn on her wedding day Gomer was awakened with a message to meet Amaziah in the inner court. She arrived first and stood in the midst of the courtyard as an early morning breeze whipped her robes about her ankles. She was awed by the splendor of the huge court where their wedding was to be held that evening.

Even unadorned the court was beautiful. A huge weeping willow hovered above a marble fountain, ascending well beyond the roof before cascading down again. Its foliage draped a replica of a golden calf centered on top of the fountain.

Aromatic fruit trees dotted the courtyard, breaking up the monotony of alternating black and white tiles, and made perfect plumage upon which to build the festive trimmings. Shimmering, weightless veils had been attached to the branches for the wedding, and they danced in the breeze. Narrow bands of scarlet were wrapped round the trunks.

At one end, a canopy of palm and olive branches, woven around a curved structure of acacia wood, encircled the couch for the bride and groom. Tables lined three walls of the court and were set with two bouquets each of bronze lilies, interspaced with baskets full of fresh tulips, irises, and poppies.

At the open end were three arched doorways overhung with green ivy. Fragrant tamarisk shrubs, already void of spring blossoms, grew at both sides. It was through this exceptionally decorated portal that Gomer would make her entrance. She inhaled deeply. *All this is for me.* The thought satisfied her.

Amaziah entered the court with Gomer's brother,

Dan, who was chatting loudly with him. "Oh, of course, he'll really be here," Amaziah said as he popped a sweetmeat into his mouth. "The king rarely misses our celebrations. Ah, here is Gomer. Come here, my dear. Tell me, what do you think of the wedding preparations?"

"It is beyond words, my lord."

"And still none of it can compare with the glory which the Lord has bestowed on you, my love." Amaziah bent to kiss her hand. "I'm sorry to tell you, but your brother has some distressing news."

Gomer held both hands out to him. "Have you come to keep me from mischief?"

"Gomer." Dan ignored her remark. "I'm afraid I have some sad news. Mother has taken ill. Her health will not permit the day's journey to Beth-el for your wedding."

Gomer said nothing. She could not believe that her mother had managed to disrupt even her wedding day.

"My dear," Amaziah took her hand. "I am sure this is a great shock to you. Is there anything I can do?"

"No, of course not. Your concern won't heal her. Perhaps you *could* send her a generous gift though. She may very well enjoy that more than attending my wedding."

"Gomer!" Dan snapped.

"She is wrought with grief," Amaziah intervened. "She's such a frail dove, the news was probably too much for her." He spoke as if Gomer were not present, although he looked into her eyes.

Gomer assumed a pout for him. She *was* slightly worried that her mother was ill enough to miss her wedding day—but the familiar irritation was stronger. After all, people take sick and recover every day. Her illness couldn't be serious or Dan wouldn't have left her.

"I will do better than send a gift," Amaziah snapped his fingers. "I will dispatch my personal physician to her at once."

"Oh, my lord!" Dan knelt and kissed Amaziah's ring. "We can never repay your kindness. It is too much."

"Nonsense. You have given me more than enough in Gomer." Amaziah lifted Dan to his feet.

Gomer noticed that Dan's eyes slid uneasily toward the fountain at the end of the court and knew what was drawing his attention.

"I see you've noticed the golden calf, brother." *My pious brother cannot overlook idolatry, even in his groveling,* she thought.

Dan's eyes bulged in warning. "I don't know what you speak of, my sister."

"You see, my lord," Gomer addressed Amaziah, "Dan is a very religious man, and he does not abide idolatry."

Dan's face grew pale.

"That is very commendable, my son," Amaziah smiled loftily. "But I hope you do not think this calf is an idol. No, no, no. It is symbolic of the seat of the living, invisible God. No, we don't worship this calf, but the one God who is Lord not only over nature but all creation."

Dan pulled himself to full height again. His eyes were filled with admiration for the high priest. Gomer was shocked at his naiveté.

"I am leaving," Gomer said with disgust. Both men looked at her in surprise. "If you have no further need of me I have many preparations to finish before the wedding."

"Of course," Amaziah dismissed her.

Gomer bowed and returned to Hodesh.

A dry summer wind attempted to blow away the scorching heat of the day. It was nearly sunset and the hour of the nuptials was nearing. The wedding guests had arrived and Gomer was waiting outside the portal to begin. She peered from behind a pillar, barely taking

41

care to hide herself. The inner court was filled with the most wealthy and influential people of Israel and Gomer strained to see them all.

The court droned with expectancy. As Gomer's eyes scanned the area she noted that the same women she had thought to be servants making perfume were seated alone at a table of high honor. At the head was a middle-aged woman whose beauty overshadowed that of the women with her.

A young priest bent to speak to her, and the two of them laughed amiably. *She is surely not a servant*, Gomer mused, as she watched the young priest affectionately kiss the woman's head before leaving. Gomer heard him say, "Shalom, Mother. We will dine together later."

Gomer was more than intrigued with the mysterious woman and her son.

"Hail, friend," a guest called to Amaziah. "If your betrothed tarries much longer, we may not see her for the darkness of night."

"Do not worry," said Amaziah. "Her beauty is such that it alone will brighten the night."

At that moment musicians heralded the wedding processional. Gomer hurriedly surveyed herself and banished all thoughts but of the wedding.

When the procession reached the portals Gomer appeared from the shadows. Complete silence fell upon all. Although it was customary to honor the bride in such a manner, this silence was more. Her beauty alone could not cause such a tumult of emotion. Though she was radiant, Gomer's beauty did not excede that of other beautiful women.

It was as if she carried with her the aura of intrigue. Something about her, like an indiscernible scent, aroused in men the excitement of a hunt, the challenge of war that surged through a man's veins as he stood ready for battle. Her presence filled the room with heady desires, bringing to life longings that set the scene for revelry, and making one feel those desires with the strength of a lion.

Gomer was aware of nothing except the admiring stares of Amaziah and every other man in the court. She was the center of all this night, just as she had always dreamed, and she fed upon it.

Turning her attention back to Amaziah, she boldly met his eyes. When he only stared like a fool, Gomer whispered, "Amaziah, take my arm!"

Amaziah quickly complied. He seemed grateful to be freed from Gomer's brazen gaze. Offering his arm, he led her to their places.

The young priest who had talked with his mother rose in greeting under the canopy. He appeared startlingly clean amid all the grisly bearded, older men in the court.

"Gomer, I am very proud to present Shema, son of Mara, the priest of the highest order, after myself of course, and newly appointed priest of the high place."

So Mara is the name of his mother, Gomer was pleased to learn.

"I am most honored," Shema said with distant formality, but in his gaze there was unmistakable desire. He poured oil from a ram's horn and intoned a blessing on them both.

Turning to the court he spread his arms out to the guests. "Honored friends of the king's chapel, I am most pleased to announce Amaziah, the high priest of Israel, and his new bride, the lady Gomer." With those words Gomer and Amaziah were joined in marriage.

The evening's opulence whirled around Gomer too

quickly. Highly glazed pottery overflowing with bananas, oranges, persimmons, jujubes, dates, figs, grapes, and pomegranates circulated without end. Small plates of olives, almonds, and pistachios placated everyone, while the mouth-watering aroma of roasting fatted calves and sheep promised to satisfy their hunger.

In addition to the ever-flowing wine, an abundance of large gourds filled with iced water of rose were served. Refreshing syrup-water made from the sap of palm trees, a favorite of Gomer's, passed among the guests also.

Though the celebration was in her honor, Gomer felt frustrated amid it. There was such riotous carousing she was eventually ignored. The wedding became simply an excuse for abandonment, and the uproar never waned, even when she reluctantly retired with Amaziah.

There was but one lamp burning in Amaziah's chambers. With the celebration roaring in the background, Amaziah beckoned to his new bride with open arms. As his damp hands caressed her, Gomer recalled with less assurance how certain she had been that the marriage upon her husband's bed would be a success.

His touch incited no passion within her. Amaziah seemed not to notice her at all, except that she was the gratification of his desire. She was repulsed by their union.

3

They have sown the wind and they will reap the whirl-wind.

Hosea 8:7

Gomer breezed through the portals into the courtyard crowded with guests, fully refreshed from the previous night's disillusionments. She had resolved not to be ignored at tonight's feast.

Before she decided how to make her presence known, she heard Amaziah clap his hands to gain the court's attention. In the silence that followed Amaziah shouted, "Greetings, my beloved guests. We have a noble visitor from the king's court."

Proudly he swept an arm toward a rugged stranger seated to his right. "This courageous general aided King Jeroboam in the siege of Damascus. All hail Menahem, loyal subject of the king."

Amid the cheers, Gomer watched Menahem's demeanor change abruptly. He had seemed displeased, even bored, but as he stood beside Amaziah to receive the adulation of the people, he looked more than pleased. He smiled and nodded.

45

Then, slowly, as they perceived Gomer's presence, the people's shouts subsided and they turned their heads from the general. He scoured the court to find a reason for their distraction. Gomer felt his eyes fall on her.

After allowing him to scrutinize her and the incomparable power she exerted, Gomer met his gaze. The man seemed to relish her with his thoughts. It surprised her that she could do the same.

He was outfitted in clothing suited to the royal court: a knee-length embroidered tunic of rich purple and gold. A sash girded his waist and carried his jutting sword. A black cloak, held by golden shoulder clasps, hung in loose folds down his back to mid-calf, where it met tight-fitting leather boots that laced in front.

He was a picture of grandeur, but the apparent stateliness of Menahem had little to do with his courtly attire. Indeed, his authoritative air made the elegant clothing seem merely an afterthought.

He wore a crisply chopped beard that outlined a firm jaw, beneath black hair that curled behind his ears and down to his shoulders. In response to Gomer's gaze his long nose flared and his full lips narrowed. Only his eyes remained warm amidst an otherwise cool aloofness. Like two refreshing oases, his deep ebony eyes radiated a promise of friendliness. But their charm was only a mirage, sapping the strength of those who were deluded by their lie.

His rugged features and attire reflected a manliness Gomer had never known but for which she had always hungered. She sucked in her breath as the realization hit her. *He is my phantom lover!*

Gomer moved past Menahem to her husband's side in an attempt to mask her growing excitement. Uncertain with her new feelings, she reverted to childish games and pretended not to have heard the salute to the general. "Have I missed something? Why has the music stopped?" Her words, though spoken to Amaziah, were meant for Menahem.

"My dear, our honored guest has arrived—Menahem, the king's loyal general and confidant."

Gomer followed Amaziah's gaze to Menahem. "The *general?*" She spoke with feigned disappointment in her voice and looked back at Amaziah as though he had denied her a favorite toy. "You said the *king* was to be here."

Menahem pulled himself to full stature. "You must be Gomer, the *child* bride of Amaziah," he leveled at her.

Gomer eyed him suspiciously. Obviously he had mistaken her teasing for an insult. She was caught off guard only momentarily. Convinced she was a match for any insolence she summoned up her own form of cunning.

"Yes, I am Gomer," she bowed stiffly. "The *young* bride of Amaziah. How is it that a man such as yourself, *so far removed from youth,* looks down upon it?"

Menahem narrowed his lips before forcing them into a smile. "Children are most dull when they believe they are not. In the future, when you bear a child, I pray you will take care to instruct him in the ways of *respect* toward men of high honor."

"No, sir. I intend to teach my children to respect those men deserving of honor and to pray for all others."

Gomer felt confident that she had finally penetrated his invincibility. Her insults had wounded his vanity.

The general's jaw became taut and his warm gaze turned to ice. The threat in his eyes was unmistakable. Amaziah nervously interjected, "How unfortunate the king has been delayed."

"Yes, quite unfortunate. Pressing matters of state prevent his attendance. He appointed me in his stead."

"For what purpose?" Gomer spoke slyly.

"To make apology for his absence."

"Apology accepted," Gomer smiled victoriously, then quickly changed the subject. "Oh, Amaziah, *do* bring the wine you specially prepared for me last evening. It made me feel as though I had just bathed in fresh spring water."

Though Gomer had won the battle, she felt a need to clear her head of Menahem. She had grown weary of the man's obvious self-centeredness, never dreaming it was so much like her own. Yet, his presence was overpowering.

Amaziah held out his hand to her. "Come, my dear, and you may watch as I prepare it."

They left the room arm in arm. When the newlyweds returned later, Gomer was noticeably drunken. By the time they reached the couch where Menahem sat, she was unencumbered by social formalities.

Gomer clung to her husband's arm for balance and spoke loudly to Menahem. "What are you staring at?" She turned to Amaziah and held her goblet upside down in his face. "My wine is all gone."

"It seems my bride needs a little rest. If you will excuse us, General . . ." Amaziah offered a weak apology. He was interrupted by Gomer, who freed herself of his arm and tried to keep herself aright. Holding her head with one hand seemed to help a little.

"Make no excuses on my behalf, husband," she pouted. Squinting at Menahem she said, "So you think I am a child?"

Menahem smiled when Amaziah attempted to restrict Gomer's movements and she flailed at his arms. Finally she fled from him, scooped up the lower portion of her dress, and jumped on a low table before he could stop her. She said determinedly, "This is what a *child* can do."

Flinging her dress around her knees she danced in the sight of all, a suggestive dance that should have been meant only for her husband. But in her state she could maintain poise only a few moments without faltering. She slipped on the table and landed almost gracefully in a heap on the floor. More than a few guests could not hold back their mirth. Menahem seemed delirious with pleasure. She had created and lost this battle by herself, without his making a move.

Amaziah had Ka'Tan carry Gomer to his chambers and followed closely behind, too embarrassed to apologize.

It took a long time for Gomer to fully waken from the intoxicated sleep. Her head swam with jumbled scenes from the evening before. Slowly the scenes brought themselves into formation, lining up into proper sequence.

Curse him! Gomer thought as she pounded a nearby pillow. The action accentuated the pounding in her head and awakened Amaziah.

"How do you fare this morning, my sweet?" Amaziah mumbled groggily.

Gomer only glared at him.

"My love, are you concerned about last night?" Amaziah turned toward her. "Do not worry. It seems you have not offended the general after all."

"I *meant* to offend him as much as he offended me!" Gomer retorted.

"After you, ah, retired last night, a messenger arrived from the palace and Menahem left in haste. I hurried to the gates to say my farewells. I told him I knew you would be most grieved that you missed his departure. He was not angry, my little turtledove, for as he rode out through the gate I could hear him laughing loudly."

Gomer kicked furiously at a pillow.

The wedding feast was over, and as was customary, Gomer had been sent to the wives' quarters. The morning quiet lingered in the chapel hallway until the stillness was shattered by a pleading cry. "Mistress, consider the outcome of your anger. You cannot return to him unless he bids you!"

Heedless of Hodesh's warning Gomer stormed out of her quarters. She was as controlled by the passion of her anger as she was by the passion of her dreams. Hodesh had to run to keep pace with her determined strides. Gomer's face was cast bronze, and her eyes burned with the intensity of a smelting furnace. Hodesh knew she must be stopped before she reached Amaziah's apartment. "Quickly! Fetch Ka'Tan!" Hodesh screamed to a nearby servant.

Amaziah was jolted from his slumber by the scuttle of Ka'Tan stumbling into his chamber. He closed the door quickly and leaned upon it. Ka'Tan was dressed in only a light linen tunic, and not being girdled or bathed, appeared as if a gale had blown him from his bed and deposited him there.

"Forgive this intrusion, my lord," Ka'Tan said breathlessly, "but Gomer seeks your audience. I sent word for her to tarry until you have washed and come forth, but she is, ah, most anxious to be admitted."

Before Amaziah could respond, Gomer's voice shrieked outside the door. "Out of my way, fool! Out of my way! I said I will see him *now!*"

"Open to her" was all Amaziah said.

Gomer burst into the room, followed quickly by Hodesh and two manservants in awe. Her presence held the promise of stimulation as did the west wind at summer's end. But as the west wind she also held the threat of sudden clouds and rain driven by the force of a gale, sending even kings scurrying for shelter. She stalked angrily to the foot of Amaziah's bed.

"May the gods curse you, Amaziah!" The blush of modesty had never touched Gomer's cheeks, but they now burned scarlet with rage. "You have deceived me. I am but one of many wives in a harem!" She spat on the floor, glaring at her husband.

Amaziah dismissed everyone but Gomer, and even Ka'Tan seemed grateful to be allowed escape. Then the high priest rose from his bed, giving a weak smile but keeping the width of the bed between them. "You flatter me with your jealousy, my love, but I see no reason for you to speak with such a disrespectful tongue."

Gomer spat again in response. Her glare was as threatening as her stance.

Amaziah nervously cleared his throat. "There has been no deceit," he went on. "I have never said I did not have other wives. I did not even know you were ignorant of them."

"You have deliberately kept it from me," Gomer shouted. "That is the same as a lie. I would not have expected such treachery from a priest!"

"Hold your peace, wife!" Amaziah said sternly.

"I will not. I would never have given my consent to be part of a harem, locked away with other women until you call for me!"

"Do not blame me that you entered marriage in such naiveté," Amaziah said defensively, then stopped short, looking relieved. "Is that what troubles you? Are

51

you fearful that I will not bring you to my bed often?"

Suddenly Gomer realized the potential danger of her situation. Had not Amaziah's conceit caused him to interpret her temper as flattery, she could even now be in disfavor, or worse yet, divorced. The thought of returning to her old life quickly changed her attitude. She stepped gingerly around the bed to Amaziah's side and fingered the belt of his tunic. "Wouldn't you feel the same in my place?"

Amaziah's belly heaved under her hand as he laughed. "I see the canopy of marriage has wakened in you a blazing fire. Would you be comforted if I shared my bed with you again this night?"

Gomer was incensed at her discovery, but she now had her wits about her. She must live with the situation and gain what advantage she could. "Yea, my lord, tonight and every night." She caressed Amaziah's lips with her finger.

"But, husband, let me stay in my chamber. Do not send me again to the chamber of your wives. The sight of those women inflame me so that I think I may die. Please allow me to remain in the separate bridal chamber."

Amaziah held Gomer by her shoulders and looked into her beseeching eyes. Gomer knew he could refuse her nothing.

"It will be granted to you," he said finally.

With a squeal, Gomer reached through the folds in his robe and patted his bare flesh. Amaziah's eyebrows shot up, to the delight of Gomer.

"Do I have your word that I will see you tonight?" she asked playfully.

"Nothing could prevent it," Amaziah said. As he walked her to the door with his arm about her waist he strutted noticeably. Gomer was amused.

When Amaziah opened the door, Gomer saw Ka'Tan lying prostrate on the floor as though anticipating his master's wrath.

Amaziah kissed Gomer upon her nose and said, "I will call for you at sunset. We will sup alone in my apartment."

The door shut and Gomer was alone with Ka'Tan. She smiled with feigned haughtiness and, jerking her robe over her arm in the manner of an Egyptian garment, marched off.

Ka'Tan jumped from his position and raced to her side. "Tell me what witchcraft you induce, and I will pay you richly for it." His laugh echoed in the hallway.

"Did you think I was a fool?" Gomer said slyly, still making pretense at arrogance. Then she stopped and grabbed Ka'Tan's arms like a childhood conspirator and snickered.

With a snort Ka'Tan quickly covered her lips with his forefinger as he looked stealthily at Amaziah's door. They were unable to contain their mischief and erupted into giggles, loudly shushing one another as they continued down the corridor.

"Oh, and you may command that the bridal chamber be converted into my permanent dwelling."

At this Ka'Tan halted mid-step. Again running to catch up to her, he questioned, "Is this the order of Amaziah?"

"It is."

"Truly I wonder at the spell you have so quickly brought upon my master." Ka'Tan blew his breath out in a whistle. As he looked intently at her, Gomer saw not only admiration in his eyes, but a spark of concern lurking there, too. She chose to ignore the warning in his eyes.

"Ka'Tan, *do* have my things moved to my private quarters now."

Ka'Tan's bow was an exaggerated gesture. "Yes, *master*," he teased by emphasizing the word. But he clapped, and two servants ran to obey.

Gomer slapped his lowered head playfully and grinned as Ka'Tan backed away from her, bowing.

On her way to her room she passed the wives' quarters and stopped when she heard Mara questioning one of the servants.

"What is your business?" Mara asked him.

"On the order of Amaziah, we are removing Gomer's things to the bridal chamber."

"For what purpose?" Mara's eyes widened.

"It is to be the private chamber of the Lady Gomer."

Mara slowly lifted blazing eyes to the doorway, where Gomer leaned assuredly. She spoke to her through clenched teeth.

"Do you think you are so far above us you deserve separate lodging?"

Gomer only lifted her chin in silent assurance.

Mara stepped threateningly toward her. "Be warned. I have not held the position of the favored wife of Amaziah for twenty years to step aside now for a young whelp!"

"Oh? Then tell me, favored wife, how will you prevent it?"

Mara fought for control but said nothing.

Gomer grinned ominously. "I will make Amaziah forget your name. And we both know I can do it." Holding herself proudly erect Gomer retired to her private chambers.

4

I appointed the prophets to guard my people, but the people have blocked them at every turn and publicly declared their hatred.

Hosea 9:8

With winter past, Beth-el seemed to resurrect itself. As the morning sun stretched its light across the spring sky, the arm of activity stretched its muscles across the entire city. Latticed windows opened to daylight. Dogs barked at the feet of playing children. Maidservants rushed about delivering messages and completing chores. Beggars positioned themselves at favored locations.

Eager to begin a new day, the marketplace merchants busied themselves setting up their stands and arranging their wares on the ground. They chatted about daily news of the city and affairs of trade. Soon they were proudly displaying their goods to customers, persuading them to purchase the finest cloth or the tastiest figs. Arriving before the midday heat, Syrian and Egyptian caravans converged upon the city from opposite directions to trade their country's goods.

By mid-morning Beth-el was an overwhelming blend

of colors, noises, and smells vying for attention. Sun-brightened reds, blues, purples, and subdued rainbow-hues flashed from every market stand and on every passerby. The aroma of freshly baked bread competed with the distinctive stink of fish, while dozens of dialects mingled with the raucous sound of merchants hawking their goods. The whining music accompanying a small band of dancers added to the noise and made it impossible to hold a conversation without shouting.

Gomer sighed. She could no longer share in the vivacious scene before her. Leaning idly against the open gate of the chapel, she remembered the days when she too was a part of life within the city. Now she could only watch with envy as the peasant women hurried through the streets with baskets on their arms and tall stone jars balanced on their heads. Gomer had thought wealth and prestige would make it possible to obtain freedom, but she had found her marriage to be only another prison, keeping her from beckoning dreams.

"You have servants to purchase all your goods," she remembered Amaziah answering when she troubled him about going to the marketplace. "My dove, I live to lay the world at your feet. I will send to the marketplace at Beth-shean and seek out rare treasures from across the Great Sea to placate your desires. But for you to mingle in the lowliness outside the chapel is to drag a silken robe through the dung."

I must think of a way to persuade him, she determined. She was about to go back inside when a strange commotion from the marketplace aroused her attention.

A young priest who had been in the sanctuary offering sacrifices had also heard the noise and joined Gomer at the gate. It was Shema, the son of Mara who had so caught Gomer's attention at the wedding feast. He stood beside her now, wondering at the cause of the disturbance before them. Gomer smiled to see that even wrinkles of concern could not age his boyish face.

"What has drawn everyone to the marketplace?" he asked with exaggerated formality. He always spoke with her so, Gomer suspected, to disguise his attraction to her. When she simply shrugged her shoulders, he said, "Let us see," and escorted her out of the chapel into a crowd of people already scrambling toward the city gates.

Gomer's heart soared once they were outside the confinement of the chapel. No matter what the trouble, she was thankful for the momentary freedom. As they neared the city gates, the noise grew riotous. Gomer looked to Shema. "Could it be that the New Moon festival has begun?"

Shema shook his head, "It cannot begin until sunset. Besides, it is always held in the high place, not in the city."

When they forced their way to the source of the commotion, Shema halted. "By the stars, I thought we were rid of him!" he mumbled, furrowing his brow.

"Who?"

"His name is Amos. He is from Judah, but he delights in coming into Israel to sting our ears with his judgments." Shema pointed to a man who stood on a bench in a row of stone benches lining the city wall. He was short, gray at the temples, and looked pathetically thin in a gray robe, slung carelessly over a tattered brown tunic. To Gomer he seemed as harmless as a wild onion shoot that did no other damage but to leave a bad taste, but he obviously riled Shema and the other citizens.

The growing crowd pressed itself upon Gomer and Shema, forcing them together. Gomer could feel Shema's eyes on her. From the beginning, his desire had been obvious to all but her own husband. She could not decide what to do with his attraction to her, so she regarded him with the same aloofness that he posed toward her. The difference was that Shema's yearning eyes forever betrayed his act.

"He is not greatly esteemed, is he?" Gomer noted as they watched Amos attempting to quiet the mob. He wasn't alone in the struggle. Gomer couldn't help but notice a young man, easily taller than anyone present, who waved his arms at the crowd for attention. His eyes were the blue-green of the Nile, and she thought his sandy hair lent a softness to his face as the wispy clouds to the barren mountains. He was outfitted like Amos, but upon his brawny physique, the clothes did not seem so drab. The two unlikely traveling companions finally succeeded in gaining the crowd's reluctant attention.

In a loud voice the one called Amos began. "The Lord says, 'The people of Israel have sinned again and again, and I will not forget it.' " The crowd became deathly quiet. " 'For they have perverted justice by accepting bribes, and sold into slavery the poor who can't repay their debts; they trade them for a pair of shoes. They trample the poor in the dust and kick aside the meek.' "

"By whose authority does he talk to us like this?" Gomer asked.

"Surely not God's," Shema answered with conviction. "Now you see why we have had our fill of this self-proclaimed prophet."

" 'And a man and his father defile the same temple-girl, corrupting my holy name,' " Amos went on, raising his pitch to be heard over the angry murmuring of the crowd.

" 'At their religious feasts they lounge in clothing stolen from their debtors, and in my own Temple they offer sacrifices of wine they purchased with stolen money.' You lie on ivory beds surrounded with luxury, eating the meat of the tenderest lambs and the choicest calves. You drink wine by the bucketful and perfume yourselves with sweet ointments."

"Come, Gomer, let us leave. You shouldn't be forced to hear the lies and ravings of this madman." Shema touched her elbow to escort her home.

Gomer pulled away. "No, wait, Shema, I don't want to go yet." Amos made Gomer aware of the refreshing scent she wore, extracted from rare flowers of Ceylon. *What does he mean?* she wondered. *How can the food I eat and the perfume I wear harm anyone?*

Shema looked confused. "Surely you can't be considering his wild accusations?"

Gomer did not answer but listened intently to the prophet. She sensed his piety was not of the ambivalent nature of Amaziah's.

"Listen, you merchants who rob the poor, trampling on the needy; you who long for the Sabbath to end and the religious holidays to be over, so you can get out and start cheating again—using your weighted scales and under-sized measures; you who make slaves of the poor, buying them for their debt of a piece of silver or a pair of shoes, or selling them your moldy wheat—the Lord, the Pride of Israel, has sworn: 'I won't forget your deeds!' "

Gomer was impressed with Amos' accurate description of Beth-el's elite, but the merchants in the crowd objected fiercely, and Gomer knew that unless he ceased his accusations he would cause a riot. It would not take much to incite the city, since they were already tensed for the New Moon festival. Still Amos raged on. Gomer wondered whether he was a man of little sense or one to be admired for his courage. Even more she wondered why she was concerned for this insignificant man and his friend.

"O evil men, you make 'justice' a bitter pill for the poor and oppressed. 'Righteousness' and 'fair play' are meaningless fictions to you! 'My people have forgotten what it means to do right,' says the Lord. 'Therefore an enemy is coming! He is surrounding them and will shatter their forts and plunder those beautiful homes.' " The prophet's voice was shrill in its intensity.

While Amos shouted his blistering indictment heads began turning toward the back of the marketplace. Amaziah appeared, looking very stern. The people moved aside so that the high priest could see the prophet clearly.

Look how the people reverence him! Gomer was shocked at the respect given her husband. She could not view him through a veil of holiness as they did. She knew how he discarded it as easily as he donned it.

All eyes returned to Amos to watch what he would do. An ominous snicker filtered through the crowd. Still Amos continued, ignoring the significance of the priest.

" 'You sacrificed to me for forty years while you were in the desert, Israel—but always your real interest has been in your heathen gods—in Sakkuth your king, and in Kaiwan, your god of the stars, and in all the images of them you made. So I will send them into captivity with you far to the east of Damascus,' says the Lord, the God of Hosts.

" 'I hate your show and pretense—your hypocrisy of "honoring" me with your religious feasts and solemn assemblies. I will not accept your burnt offerings and thank offerings. Away with your hymns of praise—they are mere noise to my ears. I will not listen to your music, no matter how lovely it is.

" 'Go ahead and sacrifice to idols at Beth-el and Gilgal. Go through all your proper forms and give extra offerings. How you pride yourselves and crow about it everywhere! Your sins are mounting up.

" 'Can you deny this, Israel?' asks the Lord. 'You silenced my prophets, telling them, "Shut up!" Therefore I will make you groan as a wagon groans that is loaded with sheaves. Your swiftest warriors will stumble in flight.' "

The mob grew angry beyond repair. Gomer glanced at Amaziah. His lip was quivering in wrath. The excitement she had anticipated when she first arrived at the marketplace was turning out to be different than she had expected. Gomer feared Amaziah would bring harm to the prophets. She was confused by their message, but she admired them for taking a stand against an entire city's hypocrisy.

Amos' blasts were like a final plea that preceded inevitable destruction. "Sadly I sing this song of grief for you, O Israel. 'Of all the peoples of the earth, I have chosen you alone. That is why I must punish you the more for all your sins. For how can we walk together with your sins between us?

" 'Would I be roaring as a lion unless I had a reason? I am getting ready to destroy you. But always, first of all, I warn you through my prophets. This I now have done.'

"The Lion has roared—tremble in fear. The Lord God has sounded your doom—I dare not refuse to proclaim it. Prepare to meet your God in judgment, Israel. For you are dealing with the one who formed the mountains and made the winds, and knows your every thought; he turns the morning to darkness and crushes down the mountains underneath his feet: Jehovah, the Lord, the God of Hosts, is his name."

The hostile crowd slithered closer to Amos, but the prophet never slackened his pace. " 'The idol altars and temples of Israel will be destroyed, and I will destroy the dynasty of King Jeroboam by the sword. . .' "

"Halt *there* with your treasonous words," Amaziah protested, and the threatening mob halted also. "I will not abide threats against our king. Take him captive," he ordered.

Men rushed forward to seize Amos, but his young friend climbed up beside him and laid a protective arm around the prophet's shoulder. The youth had a meek countenance, but the authority he commanded caused the mob to stop short. Gomer drew in her breath. The fear this commoner elicited was uncanny. "Do *you* reject the word of the Lord, you who are a priest?" he shouted at Amaziah.

Gomer thrilled at the youth's defiance of Amaziah. *These two are surely an uncommon pair,* she thought approvingly, as she watched the young man's determination against the high priest. His respect was obviously reserved for a higher authority than Amaziah's. She liked that.

Amos restrained the youth with a gentle touch. Addressing Amaziah, the prophet from Judah said, "Listen to this message to you from the Lord. You say, 'Don't prophesy against Israel.' The Lord's reply is this: 'Because of your interference, your wife will become a prostitute in this city, and your sons and daughters will be killed and your land divided up. You yourself will die in a heathen land, and the people of Israel will certainly become slaves in exile, far from their land.' "

The crowd hissed at the prophet. They would have stoned Amos with a look from their priest, but when Amos mentioned the word "wife" Amaziah seemed to hear no more. He turned uneasily to Gomer.

"Go home, wife," Amaziah shouted. When Gomer did not move he added sharply, "Now!"

The piercing sea-green eyes of the young man with Amos missed none of this. He watched Gomer defiantly disregard not only her husband's command, but the loving looks from the young priest at her side. She held her head high, and in the sunlight her dark hair seemed to shoot out luminous sparks of limestone. *How beautiful she is,* he thought, and wondered if this was how God saw his stiff-necked people. *She is just like Israel, ignoring both the ordinances and love of God. O Israel, when will you return the love of the Lord God?*

Amaziah turned back to the prophets. The blazing eyes of Amos and Amaziah held one another for a moment. Amaziah's eyes burned with black rage, and Amos' with the fire of the Lord.

"Imprison them both!" Amaziah pointed a fleshy finger at the prophets. Gomer objected violently, but it escaped her throat as no more than a moan.

Instantly the prophets were engulfed in human limbs, clawing and beating at them as they were dragged away. The crowd separated them, and Gomer could hear the piteous sound of Amos' fading voice calling to his friend. "Hosea! Hosea! Have faith!"

The penetrating cry tore at Gomer's heart. She felt a need to help these brave men who had dared defy the high priest. Yet she was confused. In the mouths of all the religious men she had known, the words of the Lord were empty chants. But with these two . . .

She heard the sound of muffled screams and of flesh being pounded and turned her head from the hideous scene. The cry of Amos clung to her. Like the mouth of a nursing baby, it would not let go.

Shema took hold of her shoulders. "Do not let this madman upset you. He deserves this punishment. All his words are lies. My father's house will never come to harm, and you are surely not a harlot. Finally that man will be justly punished for his treason. He will think again before he slanders the name of Jeroboam!"

Gomer looked at Shema blankly. "If they do not believe his words, why do they fear him so?"

"I think you are mistaking hatred for fear. But, please, put it out of your mind now, little Gomer," Shema soothed. "Think of the New Moon, and the sacrifice tonight. The cool air of the high place will drive such morbid thoughts from you." Shedding the cool restraint he normally used with her, Shema put his arm protectively around her and nodded toward the furious Amaziah. "I think we should return before my father rebukes you openly in the marketplace."

Gomer followed Shema's gaze with surprise. Amaziah looked ready to crush her. Quickly Shema steered her toward home, away from the dark rumblings of the marketplace. She acquiesced sheepishly.

5

They have played the harlot, serving other gods, deserting me. They sacrifice to idols on the tops of mountains; they go up into the hills to burn incense in the pleasant shade of oaks and poplars and terebinth trees. There your daughters turn to prostitution and your brides commit adultery.

Hosea 4:12–13

Gomer finished her bath in preparation for the festival of the New Moon. She thought the refreshment would help sort out the confusion of the afternoon, but still she could make no sense of it. She only knew that for some reason she admired the two prophets. Maybe it was because they had the courage to openly rebuke hypocrisy. She wasn't sure.

"Mistress, a servant has just come!" Hodesh rushed into Gomer's dressing room. "He brings word that Amaziah demands your presence."

"Tell him that I am not yet prepared to greet him," Gomer answered absently, as she stood before her mirror applying generous handfuls of cinnamon scented olive oil to herself. Doing so reminded her of the prophet's words concerning luxuries. She tried to dismiss them from her thoughts.

"I beg your pardon, my lady," Hodesh bowed lower than usual, "but the servant said your husband desires haste."

"Does he wish me to parade through the corridors naked? Tell him I will come to him shortly."

Only a few moments had passed when Amaziah threw open the door to Gomer's quarters with such force it caused Hodesh to scream and fall trembling to the floor before him. "Where is she?" he demanded. Without lifting her face, Hodesh pointed to the curtain of beads that led to Gomer's dressing room.

Amaziah slashed his way through the slithering strands, but the illusion Gomer created as she stood anointing herself in the slanting rays of the sun, her long, unbound hair falling down over her bare back and arms, brought him to an abrupt halt. The strong aroma of his favorite scent filled the room, and smoke from the burning incense curled around Gomer like a misty dream.

"I bid you good day," Gomer greeted Amaziah without bothering to lift her head from massaging the oil into her toes. "What is it that sends my eagle soaring to my quarters with such speed?"

Amaziah straightened his shoulders. "I must speak with you of your disobedience in the marketplace." His voice cracked.

"Disobedience?" Gomer echoed, keeping her head down to hide the anger that sparked in her eyes at the word.

"I commanded you to return to the chapel. You did not." Amaziah's voice was gaining volume.

"I heard the command, husband. I stayed so I could see the outcome."

"It was for your benefit that I commanded you to

66

leave," Amaziah remained stern. "You might have been harmed."

"But you disposed of the troublemakers so magnificently, my lord. Surely you would not deny me the pleasure of observing such a masterful display."

"I will have no more of your flattery or excuses."

Gomer was surprised at Amaziah's boldness. She turned her head to look at him for the first time. "I give no excuse, husband," she stated flatly, "only my reason."

Amaziah shifted his weight nervously under Gomer's steady glare. "Still it remains, you have publicly defied me. I cannot overlook that."

In a last attempt to sway Amaziah, Gomer purposefully lifted her leg to the vanity top, and with slow, deliberate strokes applied the luxuriant oil up and down her leg. With a coy smile she asked, "Amaziah, do you not care whether I am pleased?"

She had successfully manipulated Amaziah's affections, but he closed his eyes to her beauty and answered feebly. "You know that I do, but you have disgraced me publicly." With a sudden burst of strength he finished, "And you must be punished publicly."

The setting sun cast a dim shadow of the latticed window across Gomer's hardened features. The shadow must have inspired Amaziah, for after eyeing his wife once again he blurted out her punishment. "You have made yourself unfit to worship at the festival this night. You may not attend."

Almost fearfully Amaziah looked at Gomer. She hadn't moved, but her very stillness was threatening. Her murderous glare sent him scurrying out of the room, barking an order at the still prostrate Hodesh as he left. He had to command *someone*.

Hodesh crept into the dressing room to find Gomer

pacing the floor. She crossed over to the wardrobe and withdrew a warm robe. "Please protect yourself from the cold, my lady," Hodesh beseeched her naked mistress.

Gomer didn't answer but stopped pacing. She strode to her closet and took out a silken tunic. The last rays of sunlight caught the deep scarlet material and set it ablaze with color.

"Hurry, Hodesh, prepare my cosmetics. I must dress myself if I am to be ready in time for the festival."

Hodesh caught her breath. "But, my lady—" she halted when Gomer threw her a warning look. She quickly opened Gomer's cosmetics and stood near the vanity to wait until Gomer had dressed.

The scarlet tunic hugged Gomer's slim form that had rounded so perfectly in the passing months. The garment was sleeveless, with a high neckline in front, narrowing into thin straps at the shoulder. Gomer girded herself with a wide, blue leather belt clasped with silver and adorned by sapphires.

Quickly Gomer slid a three-tiered arm band over her left hand and past her elbow. The band of silver was studded with diamonds, and wound around her arm thrice before ending with a cast wildflower containing a single sapphire bud. It seemed to retain the brilliance of moonlight against Gomer's dark, oiled skin.

Hodesh helped Gomer put on silver, moon-shaped earrings, with crescents that fell tinkling against one another in tiers to her shoulders. Slipping two thin silver ankle bracelets over her left foot, Gomer shook her leg slightly to see if they tinkled adequately. Satisfied that they did, she sat before the mirror for Hodesh to paint her face.

"Give flight to your nimble fingers," Gomer commanded as she closed her eyes.

Hodesh picked up a small metal spatula from the dresser-top and dipped it into a palette containing a powder of ground turquoise and gum. She gently rubbed this into Gomer's eyelids with the spatula until they matched the color of the leather girdle around Gomer's waist. After blowing away the excess powder, Hodesh applied black antimony to Gomer's eyelashes for enhancement. Then brushing her cheeks and lips with red ocher, Hodesh was through.

Gomer hurriedly draped herself with a shawl of linen so finely twisted that its red flaxen threads appeared pink in their translucency. She turned back to Hodesh who was waiting with an ivory comb for her hair.

"Not tonight," Gomer waved the comb aside. "There's no time. I will wear that headband," she pointed to a silver band that was molded in the likeness of a viper, its head erect at the forehead. Blank ruby eyes stared out from the reptile. They seemed to mock the blank resolution in Gomer's eyes. Hodesh adjusted it over Gomer's raven hair, which hung loosely over her shoulders. The tresses streamed in the breeze as Gomer made her exit.

Pushing open the heavy door of her room, she nearly slammed into Mara. The opportunity to vex the older woman instantly lifted Gomer's dark mood.

"Oh, pardon me." Gomer bowed low and her eyes twinkled cruelly. "Are you headed for your husband's bedchamber yet again, my lady?" It was common knowledge that Amaziah had not called for Mara since his marriage to Gomer.

Mara drew her shawl closer and her eyes snapped. "As a matter of fact, I am."

Fury blinded Gomer as she stumbled out of the chapel and slashed her way past the bushes lining the path to the high place. She was not full of dreams this night, only vengeance. *I hate him! Either Mara or I will be the chief wife. He can't have us both. And I will make him sorry for this night's choice!*

Just as she arrived at the altar, the blast of trumpets announced the beginning of the New Moon festival. The fragrance of greenery that pungently filled the spring night air titillated Gomer's senses. But she resisted the comforting breeze and stood in the outer shadows, hugging to herself the rage she needed to carry out the determined promise of the night.

Carefully Gomer scanned the circle of worshipers to make sure her husband was not there, although she was prepared to defy him again if he were. *He must really be with Mara*, she decided when she couldn't find him. But she smiled at the sight of Amaziah's son, and a scheme of revenge began to form in her mind.

She watched eagerly as Shema lifted a dagger to slit the bull's throat. The flicker of burning torches glanced off the blade and sent searing shafts of light against the stone pavement surrounding the altar.

The singsong worship of the chanters to Yarhu, the Canaanite moon god, throbbed in Gomer's ears. It seemed to shout Shema's name with each beat. The thought of being with him possessed her. She felt herself submitting to the enticement.

With one quick, sure thrust Shema drew the life from the bull. The worshipers shouted. The bull's blood spilled onto the altar, and Gomer felt her own blood surging.

Slowly and almost unconsciously she began swaying to the pulsating rhythm of the chant. She danced her way into a circle of women already swirling upon the rough stones, patting out with her bare feet the desire that was rising in her.

70

Gomer was only slightly aware of the acrid aroma of burning hair and flesh from the sacrificed bull. But she was very conscious that Shema watched her closely as he wiped the dripping dagger on a piece of linen dampened with holy water. Sheathing it in its jeweled case, he retired to a solitary spot on the grass. His eyes were fixed on her.

Gomer was dancing much slower than the other women, as if to music that was born within her mind. The crescents falling from her earlobes and the bracelets at her ankles created their own music. Her eyes closed, she was oblivious to the presence of the other women. The silver snake encircling her head winked in the torchlight, and seemed to send flashes of light directly at Shema.

The maddening tempo began to falter, and one by one the women fell in exhaustion into the arms of waiting men, leaving Gomer dancing alone. The musicians slowed their music to match the tantalizing moves of her dance. Haunting moans escaped her parted lips.

Shema leaned forward, his eyes locked upon Gomer's form. Gomer opened her eyes, fastening them directly upon Shema. His breathing became unsteady. She held him transfixed within her gaze. Her dancing slowed to a pace of agonizing pleasure, and the music slowed to match it. Still her body gyrated in deliberate slow motion toward Shema. His eyes grew wide.

Gomer was now before him. She had come to a dead stop, with her arms gracefully suspended in mid-air. They stared trancelike at one another. The music had stopped and there was hypnotic silence. Suddenly Gomer collapsed invitingly before Shema, and with abandon he threw himself atop her.

The music picked up a bestial rhythm. Women screamed. Out of nowhere Mara appeared, clawing at

71

Shema and shouting through tears, "My son! My son! Think of what you are doing. Stop!"

So lost was Shema in this act that he could not respond to his mother's pleas.

"Shema!" Mara screamed. "Do not defile yourself with this harlot!"

Suddenly Shema scrambled to his feet, his boyish face filled with horror. "Harlot?" he breathed. "No! What have I done? The prophecy has come to pass, just as the prophet said, and by *me*, one of the Lord God's own priests!" His eyes filled with panic and tears. Shema stared at Gomer, who still lay on the grass, her nakedness uncovered. "Forgive me!" he begged and turned to run into the darkness. Gomer wiped her wet mouth with the back of her forearm and lay exactly as Shema had left her.

Mara dissolved into sobs on the floor of the altar, unnoticed amid the orgy of couples. There was the sound of swishing grass and Mara looked up, hoping to see Shema returning. But the sound was from Gomer and another man wallowing in the weeds.

6

No one can even live in Samaria without being a liar, thief, and bandit! . . . My people mingle with the heathen, picking up their evil ways; thus they become as good-for-nothing as a half-baked cake! . . . Their hearts blaze like a furnace with intrigue.

Hosea 7:1,8,6

Gomer quickly finished her packing. Impatiently she fumbled with her jewelry and glanced again at the doorway. Hodesh hurriedly entered the room.

"Well, is it true?" Gomer was apprehensive.

"Yes, my lady."

"Are you sure?"

"Yes, I heard it directly from Mara. Shema declined the king's invitation. He will not leave his room."

"And what of Mara?"

"He still refuses to see her or anyone."

"This is insane!" Gomer stomped her foot. "He hasn't left his room in weeks."

"No, my lady, not since the night of the New Moon festival."

"What do you mean by that?" Gomer demanded angrily.

"*Nothing*, my lady," Hodesh insisted. "I only speak what I have heard others speak."

"What others?" Gomer glared at Hodesh.

"I have heard Mara say things. She is most angry with you."

"Why? Surely *I* am not blamed for Shema's idiocy?" Hodesh looked at the floor, and Gomer knew she was held responsible.

"Is it because of me that Shema chose not to officiate as priest any longer?" Gomer ranted. "Why, that is ridiculous. What has a woman to do with such matters? How can I be blamed that the man refuses to attend the king's birthday? He is a free man. I do not make his choices for him." Her eyes pierced the handmaiden. "Tell me what Mara has said."

Hodesh's voice trembled. "My lady, if it please you, I would not like to repeat such slander."

"Tell me!" Gomer commanded.

Hodesh jerked to a bow. "My lady, Mara believes her son suffers such guilt over . . . over . . . that is, since the night he attended the New Moon festival, that he no longer feels worthy to serve God as a priest."

Gomer paced the floor. So she *was* being blamed for Shema's strange actions. If she and Amaziah were on friendly terms again, no one would dare utter such accusations against her. *I will have to win back the oaf's affection*, she decided. *And this trip to Samaria is the perfect opportunity.*

"Please, my lady," Hodesh approached her pacing mistress. "Try to put this matter from your mind. Besides, you have more immediate matters that require your attention." Hodesh waved her arm over the packed bundles waiting to be secured to the camels.

Gomer looked at Hodesh. Hodesh was not a common handmaiden. "You are right," Gomer gestured decisively. "I have been invited to the king's birthday, by the king himself, and I will let no one spoil it for me." With that resolve her entire countenance brightened. "By the gods, I am going to Samaria!"

Hodesh smiled broadly and urged Gomer to hurry. The camels were nearly ready.

In the courtyard the bristling activity vanquished the heaviness that clung to Gomer. Hodesh gave their packs to a servant, and the two women climbed the stool beside their camel into a miniature tent balanced atop the kneeling beast. Gomer was not looking forward to traveling in the uncomfortable sedan chair, but she was thankful the sun's direct glare was eliminated.

She was relieved to see that the two prophets, Amos and Hosea, who were in chains at the rear of the caravan so they could be tried in Samaria for treason, seemed to have recovered from their flogging. They were smiling. *How can they be happy in bondage?* Gomer marveled. Her eyes were drawn to Hosea. He was not handsome, yet there was an attractiveness about him she had seen in no other man. Why did he interest her? She knew her feelings had nothing to do with desire.

Ka'Tan signaled to his master that all was ready. The caravan pulled out, heading east. Soon they intersected with the great north-south watershed road and steered north.

Gomer watched everything like an impulsive child, her head sticking out the side curtain of her chair. She breathed deeply. *Samaria.* Even the name sounded heavenly and full of promise. She closed her eyes a moment to daydream of the empyreal capital. Any thoughts of Shema or Mara evaporated with the coolness of the morning. Gomer felt as if she were on the precipice of realizing her childish dreams. She had never given up the pursuit, and now they seemed almost within reach.

The day was bright and beautiful, and the sun illuminated the foliage along the roadside brilliantly. At the intersection of the watershed road they passed an acorn tree, easily the largest landmark for miles. It towered one hundred feet above them and covered the road with its delicious shade. Gomer reached out and grabbed armfuls of its leaves. Giggling, she tossed them around the inside of the sedan and on Hodesh's head. The servant was embarrassed at the playfulness of her mistress and blushed.

"Have you journeyed to Samaria before?" Gomer asked as she impishly dumped the last handfuls of leaves on Hodesh. Their fresh scent made Gomer tingle with anticipation.

"Only once, my lady," Hodesh answered with a tone of formality. She held onto the sides of the sedan chair to keep a semblance of balance in the exaggerated swaying of the camel's gait.

"Tell me about it," Gomer pleaded. "Everything!"

"Well, nearly ten winters past," Hodesh reluctantly began, "King Jeroboam made a religious pilgrimage to Beth-el, and Amaziah bestowed an exceedingly generous gift on the king. In gratitude he gave a banquet to honor Amaziah, and I accompanied them as handmaiden to the lady."

"Which lady?"

"The Lady Mara," Hodesh answered hesitantly.

"I was not aware you belonged to Mara."

Hodesh nodded.

"For how long?"

"Until you arrived, my lady," Hodesh nearly whispered.

This new information shed additional light on the reasons for Mara's hatred. Hodesh was a valuable possession to lose. But Gomer was too excited about Samaria to worry about such issues now. She shrugged thoughts of Mara away impatiently.

"But what of Samaria?"

Hodesh seemed relieved that Gomer had changed the subject. "It is the land of enchantment," she said in a reflective tone.

"What do you mean?" Gomer urged with unusual intimacy.

"There was a certain cook at the palace who was quite taken with me, my lady," Hodesh reluctantly confided.

"No!" Gomer reached out with a laugh and touched Hodesh's arm. This new dimension of romance added to her excitement. She felt fresh and alive again, and momentarily was willing to be on friendly terms with her servant.

"Forgive me for interrupting the history of Hodesh's conquests," Ka'Tan pulled the curtain aside as he kept pace from atop his camel, "but I wondered if you needed anything. Although from what I just heard I would say that the Lady Gomer needs to beware, or the Lady Hodesh will steal from her the admiration of all Israel." Ka'-Tan winked.

Gomer giggled and the reserved Hodesh blushed obligingly for Ka'Tan.

"Since you have inquired," Gomer leaned toward him,

"I *do* have need of something: to get to Samaria! What are these camels doing, treading a winepress? They stomp and stomp and we seem to go nowhere!"

Ka'Tan was suddenly tender. "Why must you always run to the new, my child? The new is not necessarily better. It is the old and familiar that is dependable."

The serious turn of the conversation flustered Gomer. "And what is so desirable about the dependable?" she scoffed.

The huge Ethiopian sighed. "I suppose to the young it is dull. But mark my words, when there is no longer anything new, the old and familiar *is* desirable."

Gomer poked Hodesh. "When did our head servant become a sage?" she teased.

"Oh–ho! It is disrespect that is my reward, is it? And just when I was bringing you this." Ka'Tan held up a bulging wineskin, while a torrid sun highlighted the glowing teeth his big smile exposed.

Suddenly Gomer was quite thirsty and began grabbing at the wineskin he kept just out of her reach. In feigned frustration she hurtled the many leaves in the sedan at Ka'Tan's head.

His arms protecting his face, Ka'Tan laughed. "Enough! Why do you bother with me when you have a full wineskin hanging outside of the chair?"

"I knew that!" Gomer pretended as she uncorked the forgotten bottle. She drank deeply before passing the skin to Hodesh.

The rest of the day wore exceedingly slow. The heat rose until no one cared to indulge in conversation. Even Gomer's anticipation could not lift her spirit as the torturous day continued. She paced incessantly when the company stopped for a midday meal, taking not a bite herself, and was thankful when the caravan did not stop for an evening's repast.

At sunset they neared the city. Gomer's excitement grew at once to a fervor and increased when she spied what looked like a sparkling limestone crown perched atop a plump, emerald pillow of earth. Fully blossomed spring wildflowers covered the hillsides like the ruffles of a royal cushion.

Following her gaze, Hodesh pointed. "Behold, my lady, Samaria!"

Samaria sat majestically on an oval hilltop, isolated from the mountains that towered above it on three sides. It was visible only from the caravan's position at the point where the city was joined to the east road by a saddle of land.

They entered through the main gate. Inside the massive double walls with defense towers and bastions looming overhead lay the marketplace, larger and louder than Beth-el's. There were many skin shades and eye shapes, depicting the differing nationalities of the merchants, traders, and travelers who passed through the city—so many that at first glance one would not guess Samaria to be a Hebrew city.

Gomer's party quickly passed through the marketplace and the lower end of the city where the common people lived. As they wove through the narrow, winding streets, Gomer ignored the filth she saw all around her. She had fallen in love with the city at first sight and would not admit to any blemishes.

Nearing the elevated west end that occupied the palace, the homes became larger and more elegant. The caravan turned at the corner of a building and suddenly the double walls of the palace loomed directly before them like huge, roughly cut chunks of granite, more fortress-like than majestic.

Once inside the walls Gomer was whisked away and deposited in her quarters with Hodesh before suspecting the servants had purposefully rushed their party.

"Do you feel as if we have been cast aside?" Gomer asked. Hodesh, wearing a puzzled expression, simply nodded.

Gomer opened the door and inquired from a passing servant the way to Amaziah's room. To Hodesh she said, "I will ask him what is happening," and she scurried down the hallway, her cloak billowing behind her.

Ka'Tan answered her knock and her question. "The master was called by the king as we entered the room. I am instructed to wait until I hear from him and then take you to meet him at the banquet."

"Did he say how long that would be?"

"No, but allow me to suggest you make haste to prepare yourself, lest he call for you while you are still bathing."

Gomer took Ka'Tan's advice. After draping and adorning herself with the finest she owned, Gomer had a moment to think while Hodesh styled her hair.

"Something is afoot," Gomer contemplated aloud.

"Of course, there is," Hodesh smiled. "A festival."

"No," Gomer tapped her index finger on her chin. "There is much more than that."

"I don't know what you mean, mistress."

"Nor do I, really. But doesn't it seem strange that the king would bid my husband to him before he could wash or dress?"

"Your husband is an important man, my lady," Hodesh reminded her. "I see nothing out of the ordinary in his reception."

"Perhaps you are right. Still, I feel there is something afoot."

"My lady, men are forever involved in mysterious, solemn matters. But my lady was invited to enjoy the festivities. May I bid you put this mystery from your mind and enjoy more pleasant thoughts?"

"You are wise, Hodesh," Gomer patted her hand. "And I will do as you bid."

Gomer tried to relax. For the first time she took note of the exquisite luxury of her quarters. Even the lamps were not sitting in ordinary wall niches but were hung with beaded strands from the ceiling. Gomer pointed to them. "If each lamp were lit, night would be as day."

Hodesh had completed Gomer's preparation and nodded her agreement as she absently straightened the jars, bottles, and utensils.

Gomer knelt and ran her hand over the rich carpets that were scattered abundantly. "I have never seen a guest room with both carpets *and* tiled floors."

Hodesh stood at the dressing table. It was then that Gomer saw the restless look in her eyes, and she understood the source.

"Ah, Hodesh," Gomer spoke with deliberation. "I have an important errand for you."

"Yes, my lady," Hodesh bowed.

"I would like for you to go to the royal kitchen and search very carefully for a *cook* that would be pleased to give us personal attention." Gomer winked as Ka'Tan would have. "Preferably one that is *familiar* with the house of Amaziah."

Hodesh's eyes sparkled with delight. "Oh, yes, my lady." She bowed quickly and nearly ran from the room.

Gomer wished it could be as simple to find *her* love. She crossed over to the cushioned couch, pleased that she

81

could simplify someone else's search. However, the happy deed could not overpower the nagging premonition she felt surrounding the palace since her arrival. The wait for Ka'Tan's knock seemed endless. She traced ivory carvings with her finger while her foot unconsciously tapped out the passing seconds.

7

*A*ssyria cannot save us, nor can our strength in battle. . . . They look everywhere except to heaven, to the Most High God. They are like a crooked bow that always misses targets.

Hosea 14:3; 7:16

"Sit here," a surly guard commanded Amos and Hosea. "This is where you will await trial."

"But why are we being tried at night? Is the cloak of darkness meant to disguise the evil deed?" Hosea asked with boldness.

The palace guard raised his arm and struck him across the mouth. "Prisoners are not allowed to speak."

Amos touched Hosea's arm. Hosea was not yet accustomed to imprisonment, but he quickly adopted the subservient stare at the floor expected of all prisoners.

A scuttle of sandals and the swishing of linen announced the assembling of the council. The prophets could see nothing behind the curtain separating them from the council hall, but they could hear. The guard scowled, reminding them of their status, and left to stand watch in the hallway.

The prophets looked at one another. "We will speak with our eyes, friend," Hosea said softly.

Amos answered with a nod.

Hosea smiled.

As the council members greeted one another Hosea surveyed the waiting room. It was long and narrow and stuffy. Hosea assumed the vast array of spears, shields, bows, javelins, and other armaments displayed on the stone walls, were meant to intimidate the prisoners. *And so it does*, he thought.

He looked through a slit in the curtain to see the council hall. Amos poked him, reminding him of the guard outside the door, but Hosea continued to spy. Amos soon joined him.

The council hall was huge. Because the actual walls were hidden in shadow, the tall, limestone columns bordering the darkness lent an uneasy, open feeling to the hall. It was too quiet. The only sound was the restless shuffling of the men's feet. Hosea sensed there was more to this meeting than a simple treason trial.

He was startled to see an ape sitting on the king's plump lap, and noticed that no one looked at Jeroboam as he petted the head of the gibbon. The king's soft features were creased and shadowed by his oiled, shoulder-length hair.

Hosea shivered. The cold dampness of the stone walls penetrated him. He eyed the dark hearth at the far end of the room as if wishing could suddenly produce a blazing fire there. As the last rays of sunlight played themselves out, Jeroboam lit a single lamp, in a gesture meant to begin the meeting.

"We are all aware of the reason we are meeting again," the king said. His lips seemed always curled in a disdainful sneer.

Hosea watched everyone nod in assent except the high priest Amaziah. He looked baffled.

"There has been division among the high council over this matter. I respect the opinion of everyone present." The king yawned delicately. "Still, the urgency of this monstrous matter demands an immediate decision. We must decide tonight."

There was silence among the council. No one looked directly at another, yet Hosea could tell that each man was eager to have his say. Finally it was Shallum who broke the silence.

Hosea shivered anew as the man stood before the court. By his appearance Hosea knew him instantly. It was reputed that the only way this bony, serpentine creature had gained rank in the king's army was by ruthlessness. If the tales were to be believed, Shallum's treatment of war prisoners was second only to the Assyrians' torture. Hosea cringed, trying not to imagine what unspeakable evils the man had committed.

"My good king." Shallum made his opinion known by baring his arm in a salute used as a call to battle. "The general and I agree that our fate lies at the hands of the Assyrians, not the Syrians who now threaten us. Still, I wonder why he does not counsel you to wage battle with these vicious enemies.

"I think because he is afraid! Yes!" Shallum pounded his fist on the table. "Are we women, that we back off from those who would rip open beloved Israel and leave a trail of our blood strewn throughout foreign lands?

"Good king, our artillery has never been more adequate, and the men in my troop are armed and prepared to do battle. Their remembrance of the booty from our last campaign grows dim and will gratify them no longer. Assyria would make a handsome treasure upon our backs. I say, let us war, not only with the Syrians who defy us, but with the Assyrians, who think to conquer us all!"

Amos and Hosea looked at each other in amazement. No one in the kingdom knew of these threats to their country. No wonder the council met at such hours. This meeting had nothing to do with them. Hosea gripped the curtain he stared through, his pulse pounding. That was why he had been arrested on false charges. The Lord God had put him here to watch the beginning of His judgment on Israel.

Jeroboam sat slumped in his chair, his elbow bent, holding his head in his hand. His sardonic laugh was nearly indiscernible. Hosea could think of nothing to laugh about.

The ape jumped to the floor. Supporting itself with long arms, it swayed from side to side, retreating to a dark corner. Jeroboam sat up, folding his hands on the table. For the first time the king seemed to notice the questioning look on Amaziah's face.

"Forgive me, Amaziah, for not briefing you on our deliberations. But I could not send you word. We do not want the people to know until we are decided."

"I thought we were going to try the prophet for treason," Amaziah said lamely.

"Again, I apologize," the king nodded. "Let me explain. You see, our spies report that Syria is planning to take Damascus from us. But it seems our troubles are not as simple as that, for our esteemed general, Menahem, has warned us that, though we must defend Damascus, the Syrians are not our real worry. He insists Assyria is a fast-rising threat to the entire civilized world." Jeroboam appeared inappropriately amused over the whole matter.

"I'm not sure I understand," said Amaziah. "Are the Assyrians threatening us also?"

"That was our question too," said Ishbah, one of the king's personal priests.

"And a worthy question," Jeroboam patronized. "The answer is no," he addressed Amaziah once again. "But the general feels we must look beyond the immediate danger to act wisely." The king examined his fingernails, obviously bored with the discussion.

"Yes," said Menahem. "Assyria is aspiring to world power, and though we could easily defeat the Syrians alone, that is not the issue. I have proposed that we have here, in Syria's threat, an opportunity to make a strategic move to insure our future safety. If we ask Assyria to help us fight Syria as our allies, we would disarm a most powerful foe by befriending her. We would therefore remove the threat of Assyria marching on *us* after we've defeated the Syrians alone."

"But the rest of us feel," said Imnah, another of the king's wise men, "that we are quite capable of extinguishing the flame of rebellion in Syria without involving Assyria. Asking for her alliance would only convince her of our vulnerability. Then we would truly be in danger."

"And *I* say, if Assyria is the threat that Menahem believes, let us march against them first. My troops and I are not afraid!" Shallum glared at Menahem.

As Hosea eyed the general's cool confidence he thought, *I would never want to be pitted against him. Menahem is a conqueror.* Yet the king seemed to feel no threat to his authority in the face of Menahem's air of primacy. On the contrary, he openly admired Menahem.

"Don't you understand?" Menahem spoke with icy condescension. "Of course we don't need allies to defeat

Syria. But we *do* need to befriend Assyria lest *she* become our enemy, for she cannot be defeated."

"Israel must cower before no one!" Shallum erupted.

"Be realistic," Menahem sighed. "Israel cannot prevail over Assyria."

"I will never advise cowardice!"

"Silence!" the king commanded. "We are getting nowhere, and my birthday party awaits us. Despite our differences we must decide *now*." Turning to his wise men, Jeroboam asked, "Is the council decided?"

The priests bent their heads together in a final affirmation that they were of one accord. One named Amram spoke.

"We are agreed, sire. Let the campaign toward Syria begin. A delay will only allow those plunderers a chance to regain Damascus. We must make haste. It is the time that kings go forth. Let our king's banners continue to fly over Damascus, our rightful land, and we shall march, not in the name of Assyria, but in the name of the Lord our God!"

Menahem's eyebrows furrowed slightly at the opposition, but aside from that he revealed no emotion. Jeroboam turned to the captains and the general of his army: "And your counsel?"

They all waited for Menahem to speak. Menahem only watched the table before him, slowly tapping his finger on it. His very presence wrung fear even from the powerful men of the high council. Finally Menahem said, "I have spoken."

"And so have I," Shallum retorted. Hosea thought Shallum must be too much of a fool to fear Menahem.

The ape returned from the corner and resumed its position upon the king's lap. Sitting with one elbow on the table and resting its head in its hand, the ape mimicked the insipid pose of the king. Jeroboam absently patted the ape. "I take it the division among you is permanent?"

Menahem slowly rose. "If what I have spoken is not heeded, it will mean the ruin of Israel." With deliberate finality the general turned and left the council hall, leaving the haunting prophecy lingering behind.

Finally the king spoke again. "Captains, do you advise marching on Syria without an ally?"

Silently they nodded, as if they feared Menahem would hear their defiance.

All eyes were on the king. The ultimate decision of whose counsel to heed rested with him. Amos and Hosea were rigid in anticipation. The fate of them all hung on his words.

"The urgency of the situation demands that we deal first with the immediate threat. We can search for ways to befriend Assyria later." Jeroboam waved a smooth hand in dismissal. "We will march on Syria—alone—at the feast's end. But now, we will adjourn. I beg each of you to enjoy my birthday celebration!"

Amos roughly pulled Hosea back. When Hosea looked at him questioningly, Amos nodded toward the other end of the waiting room. Amaziah was bustling around the curtain and approaching them.

Overhearing the council had been an unfortunate mistake, although no one but Amaziah knew they had heard. He swished past them and jerked open the door.

"Get in here!" he hissed to the guard. When the guard was inside Amaziah whispered, "Take these men back to the prison, and let them speak to no one on the way. Make sure they tell no one what they heard here tonight." He glared threateningly at Amos and Hosea but said nothing more.

God of our fathers, prayed Hosea, *thank You for revealing to me Your hand in our arrest, but now that we have this knowledge, what are we to do?*

8

On the king's birthday, the princes get him drunk; he makes a fool of himself and drinks with those who mock him. . . . There is violence everywhere.

Hosea 7:5; 4:2

The dancing sparkle of brass lamps hanging overhead flickered in Gomer's eyes as she threw back her head in abandonment. The portentousness of the royal birthday brought the stinging words of Amos to mind. But the warnings were vague and fleeting.

The court's inner portico was garlanded with pink rosebuds and urns filled with eucalyptus. The walls beyond the colonnade held geometric ivory mosaics, some of which were designed around oval wall niches holding lamps, urns, and idols. Cast bronze tables covered with coral linens formed a circle around the portico. Reed baskets filled with willow branches and peacock feathers sat on each table. Live peacocks strutted about as they pleased.

The guests were engaged in muffled conversations, while a servant meandered through the court sprinkling water perfumed with roses at random. Squeals of ticklish delight filtered upward when the moist scent showered its target. Musicians more accustomed to heralding great personages strummed a muted melody.

Toward the center of the court a crowd gathered around Gomer. Men competed for her attention. Escorted women tried to be friendly, but the gesture was forced and futile. The luxury of the feast thrilled Gomer but could not compare to the elation she felt at being the most sought after person of the court. Even the king did not attract a larger gathering!

The musicians strummed a sure and strong herald, and Amaziah gestured to Gomer that it was time for her to be presented to the king. Gomer caught the proud look in Amaziah's eyes as he escorted her to the raised platform supporting the king's party. *He displays me as if I were a prize carcass he brought down in a hunt,* she thought bitterly.

A trumpet sound nearly deafened Gomer, and a servant bellowed, "Presenting the Lady Gomer, wife of the most holy, high priest of Israel, Amaziah of Beth-el."

Gomer drew one side of her silken dress to a full fan in a most gracious curtsy. She kissed the king's outstretched hand. It smelled sickeningly of sweet wine and sweat. "I am deeply honored, your majesty."

Jeroboam raised Gomer up. "My dear, you are quite the choicest prize to bedeck my court in many years." His slurred words were complimentary, but Gomer noticed that his keen eyes held no real admiration. "I hope you will accept my apologies for not attending your wedding."

"Of course, sire."

A tanned, muscular man seated beside the king cleared his throat. "Forgive me," the king turned to the man, his eyes softening. "Gomer, allow me to present you to Gin-

ath, warrior of the highest achievement in the kingdom."
He waved his wine cup possessively toward the soldier.

Ginath reached out and kissed the hand of Gomer, letting his lips linger over her fingers. Jeroboam's eyes darkened with what appeared to be jealousy.

Unexpectedly, the king knocked Ginath's goblet to the floor and sprayed the warrior with the contents of his own. "You are an ingrate!" Jeroboam pouted.

Ginath grabbed the king's hand and pressed it to his forehead. "No, my lord. I was only admiring her perfume. I was thinking how sweet it smelled."

The king whirled drunkenly toward Gomer. "What is your scent?"

"Cinnamon," she answered dazedly. *Why is it that I always make enemies of the royal court?* thought Gomer, frustrated at losing control over the situation. After an awkward silence she begged leave. "The honor of meeting you has overcome me. I have need to refresh myself."

Jeroboam scowled at her. "The doorservant will direct you to the room you seek."

Gomer was aware of the king's jealous glare and the stares of all the court as she glided across the banquet hall. But she did not see the figure that darted into the dark corridor behind her.

A piercing pain shot through her right arm and she was swung around harshly. "Do you esteem yourself so highly you cannot speak when we meet?" Menahem squeezed Gomer's arm painfully. His breath stank of sour wine.

"My lord, I did not see you."

"Ha! So you are a liar as well as an adulteress." At Gomer's look of surprise Menahem curled his lips wickedly. "The entire kingdom knows how you have lain with your husband's son."

The fear that had lurched in Gomer's heart hardened into contempt. Seeking to rid herself of him quickly, she ignored his comments and answered loftily, "Truly, my lord, I did not see you, so I am innocent of your accusation. Now, by your leave, I will—"

"You are incapable of innocence." Menahem firmed the grip on her arm.

The two stared determinedly at one another.

"I am capable of *anything*," Gomer warned in a low, even tone.

Menahem studied her before finally saying what was on his mind. He gave her a twisted smile. "We're past playing your insolent games. Your husband no longer wants you, so I will take you, as it should have been from the start." Pushing Gomer against the cold, rough stones of the corridor wall, he continued his threats.

"Even at your wedding I knew you were no virgin bride. Your stature was like a strong palm, and your breasts its clusters. I said, 'I will climb the palm tree, I will take hold of its stalks, and it will be mine!' " With that he pressed himself hard against Gomer.

She let loose a sharp breath from the pain of Menahem's forcefulness and wondered how she could have ever been attracted to such a monster. "Then the stalks have withered before your eyes, for I belong to another. And even if I did not, I would die before yielding to you!" Gomer spat in his face.

Menahem's face turned to granite; even the hairs of his beard were as stone. Without wiping Gomer's spittle from his chin, he forced his lips on hers, smearing the slime onto her face. He laughed viciously.

Gomer spat on him again. "You sicken me!" she spewed, squirming to free herself. "My husband will decide your fate for this!"

Menahem pinned her arms to the wall. His mouth

close to her ear, he whispered, "Do you think my power is so little that a small thing like a husband can stop me? Why, even the pious King David didn't let *that* stand in his way."

He grabbed Gomer's chin in his hand. "Look at me!" he commanded. "I swear by my sword, you will be to me like a mare among the chariots of the king, and I will hold the whip!"

"You dream, madman!" Gomer screamed as Menahem's hand clawed her thigh, but she feared no one would hear her for the noise of the feast.

"Is my lady in need of her servant?" Ka'Tan's voice interrupted menacingly.

Menahem did not release Gomer, but he stood motionless as he measured the breadth and height of Ka'-Tan. "I should run you through," he snarled.

While Menahem's attention was diverted, Gomer wrenched herself free from him and ran into Ka'Tan's protective arms. "If you sought to frighten me, General, your strategy *failed*," Gomer slung the word at him, sensing that failure was one thing Menahem could not endure.

"Forget not my words, little wolfen. For this is not the last of me," Menahem threatened, then disappeared down the dark corridor.

Ka'Tan turned to Gomer. "My lady, you must be more watchful," he implored.

"How was I to know there was danger lurking in the protective walls of the palace?"

"That is not what I mean," Ka'Tan said. He stared at the ground thoughtfully a moment before going on. "My lady, you have a way about you that threatens others in power."

"Me?" Gomer giggled but was inwardly pleased. She

was a woman who threatened people in power! When Ka'Tan put it into those words Gomer realized what had been missing in her life. It all fell into place. *Power* would put her in control of her life. The months of floundering in uncertainty were over.

"You must appease those in authority, not defy them. Had you not teased Menahem from the start this would not have happened." Ka'Tan peered at her. "Are you listening, my lady?"

"Yes, I heard you. But I think you are worried about nothing. I can care for myself."

"Like you did just now with Menahem?" Ka'Tan persisted. There may be more like him for you to contend with. Please, my lady—"

Gomer held up her hand. "Ka'Tan, I am here to celebrate the king's birthday, and so it shall be."

9

Their plot smolders through the night, and in the morning it flames forth like raging fire. . . . In one morning the king of Israel shall be destroyed. . . . Even if I gave her ten thousand laws, she'd say they weren't for her. . . . She has appointed kings and princes, but not with my consent.

Hosea 7:6; 10:15; 8:12,4

The ape's morning cry pierced the palace silence. Frightened guests ran into the hallways, Amaziah and Gomer among them. Lamps were lit. Servants attempted to assure the dignitaries all was normal as they explained the ape's usual sunrise screams. But then another scream was heard from the king's chambers that obviously did not come from the ape. Palace guards rushed through the halls, joined by Amaziah and most of the high council.

Hodesh hustled Gomer back into her room. "I think it would be best for you to stay in here until we know what is happening. It could be dangerous."

"No," Gomer stated. "I will wait in my husband's quarters for him."

In Amaziah's chambers Gomer shuddered. Grimly she gathered her shawl and sat on her husband's bed to await his return. She drew the tapestries on every side of the bed and encircled herself with a wall of cushions. There she huddled for what seemed like eternity.

Finally she heard murmuring and recognized her husband's voice in the low conversation. Amaziah sounded disturbed. The door opened, and Gomer was about to pull aside the bed curtains to ask Amaziah what happened when she heard the priest named Ishbah say, "I hope you do not mind this intrusion. But the council room is not private enough for what we must discuss."

"I understand," Amaziah said. "You are welcome. I, for one, am glad you called us together so quickly."

Gomer knew she still had a chance to reveal herself without causing embarrassment, but her curiosity held her. Even before she heard the voices of the rest of the council coming she knew she would stay secretly trapped in her cubicle.

"Noble officials," Ishbah addressed the council. "I am most saddened at the reason for our meeting together again so soon. That someone in the palace has just assassinated the king is quite disconcerting. But I think you will all agree that, unless the murderer confesses, he has succeeded in his foul crime."

Gomer's spine tingled and she drew the cushions closer. A few men sighed.

Ishbah went on. "Our king is dead, the Syrians are ready to march on Damascus . . ." Gomer nearly gasped at the mention of war, ". . . and it is our duty despite our grief to carry on in the many matters of state that the king's sudden death gives rise to."

"Honored members of the council," began the priest Imnah as he stood to address the men. "I would bring up a matter of utmost urgency. As the council is aware, while our beloved king yet lived, we begged him to appoint someone to succeed his throne." There was a murmur of agreement from the priests around the room. "But," Imnah added, "the king would not hear of it."

"That is correct," Amram, another of the court wise men, interjected. "Our lord, the king, quieted us at every mention of his son Zechariah. We warned him many times that he should make provision for an heir to his throne, since Zechariah was unsuitable. We could never understand why he would leave his kingdom in anarchy when it came time for him to sleep with his fathers."

"I perceive that I might shed light on this misunderstanding." Amaziah cleared his throat nervously. "Once, long ago, the king consulted me on this matter. I spoke to him then as I speak to you all now. Why should the king need to appoint another heir to the throne when he has his son Zechariah?"

"Do you not know the law of Moses?" Ishbah asked curtly, implying ignorance on the part of Amaziah.

"If you speak of the law that says a man must be without blemish to fill the role of priest, I am aware of it," Amaziah answered.

"That is the one," nodded Ishbah. "If you know the requirement of priesthood, how can you yet recommend Zechariah as successor?"

"Because we are not anointing Zechariah as priest but as natural successor to his father's throne," Amaziah insisted. "I am certain *you* are aware, since you also are a priest, that the tradition of the king's office being equated with the office of a priest was borrowed from the heathen. Nowhere in the books of the law is there mention of kings having to fulfill the requirements of priesthood. In fact, nowhere in the books of the law is there mention of Israel having a king. Even that tradition is borrowed from the heathen."

Gomer was bewildered at this side of Amaziah. It surprised her to hear her pompous husband speak with sincere concern about disregard for the laws of God.

"A mere technicality," sniffed Ishbah. "Since it is *now* the tradition of our people to crown kings, and, as you say, equate his office with that of a priest, then the law does apply," Ishbah said triumphantly.

"If the law applies to kings then Jeroboam should not have been king either, for the law also requires a priest be a Levite, and Jeroboam was not of the tribe of Levi!"

Leaning forward, Amaziah challenged Ishbah further. "And the fact yet remains that the son of Jeroboam has no physical blemish. Zechariah is not blind, or lame, or disfigured of face, or deformed of limb. He has no broken foot or hand, is not hunchbacked or dwarfed, has no obscurity of the eye or scabs, nor is he emasculated, as the law specifies. Or have we become so adept at changing the laws that we dismiss that one too?" Amaziah concluded with a long breath.

"Zechariah has a blemish of the mind! He has fits. That is worse!" Ishbah bellowed.

"I repeat, priesthood is not what we are proposing for Zechariah. He is the firstborn of the king. The throne is rightfully his!" Amaziah argued with conviction.

There was momentary silence in the room. Again Imnah spoke with resolution. "We oppose Zechariah's enthronement."

"Do you oppose the word of the Lord concerning Zechariah?" Looking directly at Ishbah, Amaziah spoke cunningly. "Do you not know the word of the Lord to Jehu, that his sons would rule over Israel unto the fourth generation? My fellow priests, Zechariah is the fourth generation of the house of Jehu. We have no choice but to enthrone him."

"Suppose we do," Ishbah said reluctantly. "He never leaves the apartment adjoining his mother's. The youth knows nothing about matters of state."

"Zechariah has a clear mind except when his possession strikes, and that lasts only a short while. The court has a quite capable head administrator, king's adjutant, and secretary of state. Working together, their wisdom and skill would train the new king proficiently," Amaziah finished with assurance.

The court officials had said nothing during the discussion of the priests, but now Gamaliel, the head administrator, interrupted. "Sirs, we have listened begrudgingly to your stuffy theology. Since you hold as much influence over matters of state as we do, we have no choice but to listen, but you are wasting time. Enough of these irrelevant doctrinal debates. We *must* have a king!"

There was silence in the room again.

"Gentlemen of the court." Menahem's voice carried awesome authority. "While it is true we must have a king, it is my opinion that the decision is not our first priority. We still have the imminent danger of war and the final decree of our beloved Jeroboam." Even after the king's death, Menahem continued his loyalist game, but Gomer knew better than to trust him. "Did he not order us to battle with the Syrians to hold the city he and I fought so hard together to win? We must rally the troops and go forth to carry out the last wishes of our king. A coronation can wait until we have secured the safety of our country."

There was a murmur of discussion. Amaziah cleared his throat again. "I am inclined to agree with the general. Still, there is one other little matter. The self-proclaimed prophet, Amos of Judah, did prophesy in my city that God would strike the house of Jeroboam down by the sword. I sent word to Jeroboam of the treason at the time, but because of the constraining issues of war it was never brought to council.

"For the sake of the people I advise we not let it become public knowledge how our lord, King Jeroboam, was killed, lest we give credibility to this rebel's ravings. The masses are easily beguiled, and we, of course, want to keep the name of our king righteous in the eyes of the world.

"We have always known Amos to be a madman, and to allow this coincidence to give him a following would be most detrimental. May I have the agreement of the council to send out decrees saying the king died peacefully while at rest?"

The priests and wise men quickly affirmed Amaziah's proposal, but Shallum slammed his fist upon the table and spoke for the first time. "I have patiently endured this council. But I have heard enough of your dribbling about religious trivialities," he shouted. "I care not what some village idiot preaches to the people or what the law says of deformities. One of our major cities is about to be besieged by our enemies, and our king gave us orders to go to war. *That* is the only reason I am here." Gomer could almost feel Shallum's reptile eyes glaring at the roomful of men.

"Shallum, this time you are at least partially right," Gamaliel conceded. "If our enemy is not disposed of first, a king may not be needed."

"Then is it agreed that I shall rally the troops for battle?" Menahem quickly moved in.

Everyone agreed, though some hesitantly. "Then I will issue the orders," Menahem stated, pausing, as if defying anyone to question his authority.

Gomer realized Menahem had usurped the right of the

king, but she suspected that the council would do nothing.

Amaziah recalled the attention of the council in a shaky voice. "I beg your patience for interrupting such important matters again, but may I be so bold as to request use of Jeroboam's signet ring to seal the decrees announcing the *natural* death of our king?" Amaziah had addressed Menahem since he seemed to be in control now.

Ishbah addressed Menahem also. "I think this would be most wise."

Gomer leaned forward, intent on hearing every word. She was sure power was the only means to secure her dreams, and Menahem was now the man in power. She had already alienated him, so she would have to find a way to gain power on her own. But how could a woman do that? She must listen and learn from Menahem. Amazingly she felt something akin to admiration for the cruel general.

"If it seems good to you, Ishbah," Menahem finally answered, "then who am I to oppose?" Gomer could sense a smile spreading slowly across Menahem's face. "Give the king's seal to Amaziah," he permitted with cold assurance.

The high council dispersed quickly. With the noise of the shuffling men to mask the sound of her own activity, Gomer disrobed and lay back upon Amaziah's bed as if asleep. She heard the secretary of state say he would have the guests cleared from the court and the festival called to an end.

Afterward, Amaziah shut the door and let out a long sigh. He walked slowly and heavily to the bed and drew back the tapestries.

"Gomer?" he said, shocked. When she didn't answer

he leaned close to her and whispered her name. Gomer slowly opened her eyes as if from a deep slumber and stretched luxuriously. "How long have you been here?"

"My husband," Gomer reached for him. "With all the screaming, I must confess that I was too fearful to abide within my own quarters, so I took refuge here. The protection I felt within your covers soon erased all my fear, and I slept. What is the hour? Have I slept long?"

Amaziah looked relieved. "Gomer," he said seriously, "you must return to the chapel in the morning. The king has died in his sleep."

Gomer gasped.

"And," he said, pausing before continuing, "we are going to war. I must go to bless the troops at the battle site. Normally I could do that here, but I feel they need this encouragement. I will be back soon, and if you are at Beth-el with Ka'Tan I will have no need to worry about you while I'm gone."

"You do what you must, my brave husband. My only regret is that we did not recover our love sooner. I have another confession, my lord."

Amaziah looked at her cautiously.

"You have kept me from you so long, my love. Is my punishment for my moment of madness with Shema going to last forever? I need you, my lord. And," Gomer lowered her eyelashes, "I thought that whatever was the urgent issue this morning . . . well, I had hoped that you would need me."

Amaziah could resist no more. "I do need you, my dove."

"Then?" Gomer looked up at him pleadingly. She did not wait for his response but clung to him in a pretense of enjoyment.

10

They have sown the wind and they will reap the whirlwind.

Hosea 8:7

The outer courtyard was empty. The desolation of the
chapel sent a penetrating shiver up Gomer's spine as she
dismounted at the gates. She looked at Ka'Tan. A
mournful sound came from the priests' quarters, and
they ran toward the cold stone building.

After following a seemingly endless maze through the
corridors they found the entire household huddled together in an open hall, wailing and weeping. Ka'Tan
pushed his way through the mourners and was lost to
Gomer's sight. She called out.

"There she is!" A woman's voice shrieked above the
moaning.

The crowd flattened against the walls of the corridor
to reveal Mara hunched on the floor like a beast of prey.
She slowly rose and faced Gomer, her hands and tunic
dripping with blood. At her feet lay Shema, white-
washed with death. Gomer staggered.

Mara pointed a crimson-stained finger at her. Her

104

maniacal eyes glazed. "You killed him!" she whispered hoarsely. "Just as surely as if you had thrust the sword into his heart with your own hand."

Involuntarily Gomer drew back. She searched the faces that lined the wall for a defender, but there was none. Her guilt was reflected in each face. She was sweating. "How could I have killed him?" she asked of them, but the words sounded condemning even to her own ears. "I've been at the palace," her voice trailed to a whisper.

"You needed only raise your skirt to kill him." Mara breathed her venomous accusation through clenched teeth.

"You don't still believe—"

"Murderess!" Mara trembled. "You must pay for your crime. You must die!" The screeching verdict chilled the marrow of Gomer's bones. With hellish ferocity Mara lunged for the bloodied sword still tightly clenched in the hand of her dead son. She waved it menacingly before Gomer. "Your guilt has been proven. My son took his life to atone for the sin *you* brought upon him."

Suicide. The horrid thought sucked the blood from Gomer as if the earth beneath her feet thirsted for it.

"I see fear touches your soul also." The rancor of Mara's laugh filled the corridor. "But fear will not avail you. I heard the confession from his own lips. His last breath was used to condemn you."

The tip of the sword danced tauntingly in front of her. Gomer fought hysteria. With relief she glimpsed Ka'Tan easing unnoticed into position behind Mara. *Hurry,* she wanted to shout. *The woman is bereft of reason. Stop her!*

"I will reckon with you," Mara moaned piteously and lifted the sword, only to have Ka'Tan grab her raised

105

arms and wrest it from her. "Do not stop me," she begged. "She must die as my son has died."

Frozen in her stance, Gomer grew as pale as Shema's corpse. "Then stone her," Mara desperately pleaded with Ka'Tan. She pointed a gnarled finger at Gomer. "I beg you for justice! She is the reason my son took his life. Don't you understand? You are protecting a murderess. She must pay!" Her voice rose to demoniacal pitch and she lurched forward, her fingers straining for Gomer's throat. Once again Ka'Tan interceded between Gomer and death.

"Someone help me with her," he grunted, as he fought to restrain Mara. Not a man in the house lifted a finger for Gomer's protection. The only movement was the ferocity of Mara's struggling.

"Cursed are you, Gomer!" Mara whispered a hoarse verdict. "May the gods avenge my son's death with your own!" She threw her head back against Ka'Tan's chest as he dragged her away, whimpering, "She is guilty. Don't you see? She must pay. By the gods, make her pay!" Writhing sobs racked her body, forcing her to give up the struggle. She hung limp in Ka'Tan's arms, her lifeless eyes fixed on Gomer, as she disappeared through an archway.

The sweltering arid wind swept through the corridor. It stirred the robes of each marbleized person in the nightmarish ordeal. Gomer stood alone, her body still flinching, as if a spectre of Mara lingered behind to torment her. Her senses reeled as the vision of Shema crowded her mind. Her thoughts dissolved to mere echoes, swirling, bumping against one another, knocking each other out of consciousness's range....

Gomer advanced her ivory game piece to the center

line of holes on the ebony game board. "I have won again," she said dully to Hodesh.

"I do believe no one can defeat you in *Hounds and Jackals*, my lady." Hodesh tried to cheer her.

With a deft stroke Gomer sent the game pieces flying, and Hodesh scurrying to pick them up. "This confinement has nearly beaten me! I can stand it no longer!" Her sandals clicked across the floor, and she threw open the door of her quarters. "Ka'Tan!" she barked.

At the sound of her voice the exhausted servant raised his unkempt form from the wall where he reclined and was instantly alert. He alone had stood guard at her door the past several days. "Yes, my lady," he bowed.

"Ka'Tan, I insist we stop this insanity. There is no reason to keep me prisoner here."

Ka'Tan sighed, too fatigued to go through the conversation again. "My lady, you are no prisoner. You know these measures are taken only for your protection until your husband returns from battle."

"Protection!" Gomer snorted. "From whom? An old woman?"

"Do you think the death in your meal pot found its way there without intent? Has our cook suddenly started using hemlock as seasoning? I beg to differ, my lady. This protection is not without cause."

The memory of the poisoned pot silenced her. Mara's shrieks echoed in Gomer's thoughts as lamentations bounce off cold tomb walls. She had struggled with the guilt and thought she had it conquered. But with Ka'-Tan's words she had to renew her vow. *I will not let them blame me for something over which I had no power. By the gods, I won't accept the guilt they are laying at my feet!*

"The master will return soon, my lady." Ka'Tan's

voice softened at Gomer's distress. "And when your husband is here your confinement will be over. He will be your protection."

Gomer released her breath in what resembled resignation. As she turned to retreat into her quarters she heard a distant, haunting moan. The volume increased as more voices joined in.

"Stay here, I will see to it," Ka'Tan said over his shoulder. Without hesitation Gomer followed him, too curious to stay behind. They had not gone far when a tattered soldier approached, breathless and panic-stricken. His clothes were rent and dirt dusted his hair. "Are you the overseer of the high priest's household?" he panted to Ka'Tan.

"I am. What is wrong?"

The wailing had increased to such measure Gomer could barely hear the soldier's reply. "The Syrian forces overtook us even as we made camp outside of Damascus. They had already besieged the city . . ." He paused and a pained look swept over him. "The high priest was slain."

Gomer swayed dazedly in the sedan chair that carried her to the safety of her mother's tent. Ka'Tan finally broke the silence that had surrounded them since they left Beth-el. "My lady, it is permissible for you to cry."

"What would tears accomplish?" Gomer responded tonelessly.

"Some say they have a cleansing power."

Gomer looked at Ka'Tan pointedly. "And what do you think I need to be cleansed of?" He didn't answer. Why did the subject of her guilt keep surfacing? She didn't feel guilty. She wasn't sure what feelings she harbored anymore.

Ka'Tan proposed tears for her, but she had none. The only emotion she felt at the news of Amaziah's death was fear of further confinement in her quarters, so she had chosen to abide at her mother's tent for a time. Ka'Tan encouraged her decision for it would take her out of Mara's reach.

As the camels lurched lazily toward the familiar family tent, one of the handmaidens Amaziah had given Salome rushed out to meet them. "I regret I must greet you with sadness, mistress Gomer," she bowed.

Gomer furrowed her brow.

The handmaiden took a deep breath. "Mistress Salome has gone the way of all the earth. We have buried her. Your mother died alone. Dan has been gone since the latter rains. He left for Samaria to seek a merchant's trade, taking all the wealth to establish himself. We have had no word from him since."

Gomer turned away. No emotion was evident.

"Wait," the maiden said. She ducked into the tent and came out with a brilliant red scarf in her hand. "Mistress Salome's last words were for me to give this to her daughter. She found it behind the tent. It has been tied to the center tentpole since you left." The girl solemnly tied it around Gomer's neck.

Gomer fingered the folds of the scarf. How many eternities had passed since this piece of dyed linen had been her only source of pleasure in life? The thought of her lonely mother draping it in a place of perpetual memory brought stinging tears to her eyes.

Gomer bristled inside. So the God who had taken her father from her had claimed her mother as well? Clenching her fists she vowed renewed vengeance on this bloodthirsty deity. She turned staunchly on her heel and stalked to the top of the knoll she once held sacred.

The familiar terrain melted away as her eyes searched the horizon. Gomer combed the clouds with her stare as if she would find the Lord among them and confront Him with her hatred. Her pace quickened as the short ascent steepened. Brushing past dense foliage that thickened as her rage, she burst into the clearing at the cliff's edge and was nearly blinded by the sun's glare.

Again came the familiar wind. It weakened her resistance. It caressed her burning face. She was seething with vile emotions, but the breeze called her to peace.

Peace! It was because of you, Gomer thought bitterly of her wind-lover, *that I ever pursued it. You made me believe happiness was obtainable. And what has my chase gotten me? I am orphaned, widowed, labeled harlot, and accused of murder. The more you promise, the more the Lord snatches away.*

Why did contentment beckon her so enticingly if it was so unattainable? Gomer listened to the gentle whisper a moment. Renewed hope channeled her thoughts in another direction. *The God who seems to desire only the dead has taken my wealth and power too. But am I to give up this battle so soon?*

A distinct wind arose, one that whirled about her feet, lifting her skirts. *No,* it seemed to whine. *Be strong! You have not searched in vain. You have not truly searched. You must continue. Alone.*

"Gomer!" Ka'Tan's voice was sharp behind her.

Gomer whirled to face him, shocked at his disrespectful tone.

"Your behavior is unforgivable!" he rebuked.

"And from whom am I expected to seek forgiveness and behave so favorably for?" Gomer slung back at him, surprised by the bitterness in her words.

"You mourn not the death of Shema, or Amaziah your

110

husband, *or* your mother. Your only concern in their tragedy is the consequences for yourself! You have donned the widow's garments in hypocrisy!"

"You dare to speak this to me?" Gomer demanded. "You dare accuse me of hypocrisy? I am not a priest that I seek to deceive."

Gomer paced the knoll's ledge. Abruptly she swung to face Ka'Tan. "Perhaps you are right. My husband's death does *not* grieve me. But," Gomer clenched her fists, "I was not fitted in mourning cloth for pretense. And I will not be thought a hypocrite!" She grabbed the edge of the garment and ripped it from her body. She stood in only her night tunic, glaring at Ka'Tan. "Take it away!" A sob escaped her as she threw the robe at him.

Ka'Tan scooped it up and ran the distance to the camel packs below, racing back with a handful of softly colored linen for his mistress. "Gomer. . ." His voice was tender as he handed her the bundle.

"Stop!" she commanded. "I will not abide your pity. I have no need of it. I may be destitute, but I am not overcome!" Gomer thrust her head into the persuasive wind as if to rise above her plight on its strength.

Ka'Tan approached her sympathetically. "What will you do, little one?" he asked softly, helping her into her outer tunic.

"Stop it, I say! Do not feel sorry for me. These events are my good fortune."

"But you are left with nothing." Ka'Tan spread his arms in compassion.

"I *need* nothing."

Ka'Tan shook his head sorrowfully. "You are wrong, little one. You are in desperate need of something. Of what, I know not. I wish I did." His eyes brimmed with tears.

Intense longing welled up in Gomer at the paternal regard in Ka'Tan. Her pent-up affections knotted painfully against the dam of bitterness that forbid her to return her friend's love. She turned from him and faced the wind. One moment the breeze was a searing desert blast, and the next, cool refreshment. Always the two whipped about her, buffeting her emotions between the desire to share love with someone and the gnawing hunger for excitement and enjoyment. Would she ever hold fast to one and be content to leave the other?

Her head swam with conflicting desires, but the hot breath of the sands blew a final gust in her face. Gomer closed her eyes. "I cannot return to the chapel as long as Mara is there. I must leave."

Ka'Tan grabbed her arm. "Your senses have departed! You cannot survive. Do you realize the danger of a woman traveling the highway alone? I will not permit it."

"Ka'Tan." She smiled. "I will find a way, with or without your consent. Besides, my poverty is my salvation. For what can thieves steal from me?" They stared at one another, knowing well what else a thief would desire from her.

"I will not permit it!" Ka'Tan thundered again, but the command rang hollow as he observed the resolve in Gomer's eyes.

She paced again. Ka'Tan stood by helplessly. "Of course," Gomer stomped her foot. "I will go to Samaria to find my brother. If he can escape the life that bound him, so can I. I will look for him."

"But Dan has not been heard from. He may not even be there."

"I will not know unless I seek him, will I?"

"But, my lady, alone?" Ka'Tan pleaded. "At least allow me to accompany you."

Gomer considered the huge man's offer. "No," she answered finally. "I must begin anew, unencumbered by anyone."

"This is unheard of!" Ka'Tan protested.

Gomer silenced him with her eyes. They looked at each other a long time, their thoughts too full to be voiced. Finally Gomer spoke. "May I keep my camel?"

"Of course," the servant whispered.

Gomer walked away. Turning, she looked at Ka'Tan one last time. "I . . ." her voice broke. "I am grateful for your friendship." As she walked unswervingly toward her camel she untied the scarlet scarf from her neck and let it flitter away in the sparse summer breeze.

11

They kill their kings one after another, and none cries out to me for help. . . . The Lord said to Hosea, "Go and marry a girl who is a prostitute, so that some of her children will be born to you from other men. This will illustrate the way my people have been untrue to me, committing open adultery against me by worshiping other gods."

Hosea 7:7; 1:2

"What is it, Amos?" Hosea was fearful. His eyes darted about in the darkness. He felt, rather than saw, the disgust that radiated from Amos.

"Israel has desecrated her precious hospitality! This inn has been dedicated to Baal!" Amos threw a small clay figure into the dry dust, shattering it in tiny pieces. "In Judah such idolatry would never be tolerated."

"Should we leave this place?" Hosea asked almost superstitiously.

"No, we have nothing to fear." Amos patted Hosea's arm. "Israel's idolatry can't touch us as long as we are true to the Lord God. This inn will serve us just as well as the pagans."

"Then if we're going to make camp, let me build a fire.

Our faithfulness might ward off spiritual evil, but the beasts of the field need a more visible ensign." As Hosea skirted the grounds for twigs and brush, the light of the rising moon revealed the camp to be no more than a deteriorating booth surrounded by a deserted olive grove.

At one time abundant lodges, such as this one, filled with all the provisions prospective travelers could desire, were scattered throughout Israel. They stood as a thriving symbol of Israel's kindness to sojourners. The abandonment of this inn to Baal was but one of many signs to Hosea that Israel was sinking deeper into the pit of corruption. There was no longer any cause for pride in his native land.

Hosea kindled the fire while Amos sat musing. The two remained pensive until it blazed before them. The snaps and sizzles of the flames mingled with the lonely sound of distant owls calling to one another, and the scratchings of rats and cockroaches around the campsite. It seemed an eternity before Hosea heard a faint sigh coming from Amos. He studied the visage of the prophet through an orange haze. "Is your heart still troubled?"

Amos snorted. "I cannot fathom such evil."

"Do you mean the idol you found?"

"No," Amos' voice was harsh, "though that is a great sin in the eyes of the Lord God. It is the chaos reigning over Israel I do not understand. Assassinations, injustice, wickedness, idolatry! For five years we have roamed the hills of southern Israel bringing the message of the Lord, and all the while these abominations multiply. It was not only the high priest who declared we had no jurisdiction in Israel, but all the people. They mocked not only us, but God as well."

Hosea sighed. He did not feel the anger that Amos seemed to. Instead, he felt great sadness for the waywardness of Israel. She was doomed and she did not know it.

Amos continued his condemnation. "For that reason Israel was overpowered in Damascus, even though Jeroboam's army was well known for its prowess. Israel cannot defeat the word of the Lord. It stands forever," his eyes flashed. "Joshua said if we mingle with heathen nations, God would no longer chase them away and they would become snares and traps to us, a pain in our side and a thorn in our eyes, and we would disappear from this good land which Jehovah gave us. This is the beginning of the end, Hosea."

Hosea nodded. "I've been wondering about the prophecy you gave concerning Jeroboam. Why didn't it stand? Jeroboam died peacefully in his sleep, not by the sword as you said."

"Ah," Amos leaned his small frame on one arm. "The Lord sees what man cannot." Shrugging his shoulders, he added, "I do not know, but God said He will scatter our kings, and Israel was two years without a king after Jeroboam died. His judgment is upon our leaders."

"And when Zechariah was finally crowned, he held the throne barely six months before Shallum killed him and declared himself king. Amos," Hosea's eyes widened, "do you think Shallum could have plotted Zechariah's death right in our midst, while we were being held in the palace prison?"

"Regardless, Hosea, the murders were done in the presence of the Lord. The precedent has been set and the crimes permitted. No king is safe now." Amos vehemently poked at the fire with his staff. "I am grateful that the Lord allowed us to witness the private council. It was worth the scourging they gave us before our release. Obviously Israel has deceived herself with her prosperity

116

and false alliances, but we witnessed the greatest vulner-ability of our brethren, their haughty pride."

"With all the signs and prophecies that the Lord has al-ready given, what more will it take to return them to Him?" Hosea's tone was pleading, but there was no answer.

Hosea and Amos sat quietly for some time, the hoot of distant owls emphasizing their silence. Amos took some dried figs out of his scrip and passed some to Hosea. The crumbs that dropped quickly became dinner for the boldest vermin.

"Hosea, may I be straightforward with you?"

Hosea smiled. "Of course, my friend. Whatever is on your heart, speak it."

"Hosea . . ." Amos sat in thought before he spoke. "I am only a herdsman and fruitpicker, but when the Lord called, I answered."

"So you have told me, friend." Hosea swallowed a mouthful of figs and smiled. "But I have yet to find a greater eloquence in all Israel."

Amos waved his hand and shook his head, dismissing the flattery of his young admirer. "Remember when I first came to Samaria to speak God's message, and your father invited me as a guest into your home?"

"Yes, well I remember your magnificent visions and exhortations, and most importantly your compassion for the poor. I had seen only fifteen summers but I knew I couldn't live long enough to find one truer to Jehovah than you. That was five years ago and still no one has taught me more of the Lord God than you. I will be for-ever grateful, Amos, for the godly influence of your life on mine."

"Hosea." Amos jabbed at the coals of the fire with the end of his staff. "I am white-bearded and no longer a youth. I am tired and long for my desert home. I yearn for the peace I found there. Israel wearies me." He cleared his throat and squinted his eyes at Hosea. "But I cannot leave Israel without a prophet."

Hosea thought the fire darting from the prophet's eyes revealed more than just the mirrored image of the flames.

"The Lord God instructed me to bring you with me and teach you in the ways of a prophet. But answer me in truth, has the Lord yet spoken to you the word He would have you preach?"

For a time Hosea sat in wonder at the question Amos posed. He knew the vague stirring in his heart was not what Amos meant. He had not heard the Lord speak yet. He laughed uneasily. "I did ask you to say what was on your heart, didn't I?"

"What is the answer, Hosea?"

"Well, no."

"It is as I thought. Hosea, go home to Samaria. Look for a wife. I'll remain in Israel and perhaps record my pilgrimages before the Lord bids me home. God will reveal His will to you in His season. Live as an honorable man until the time God calls to you."

Hosea laughed nervously and cleared his throat. "What need does a prophet have for a wife? You have none. Is not the Lord called *El-Shaddai*, 'God Almighty'? Therefore, is He not enough?"

Amos smiled and pointed a finger good-naturedly at Hosea. "You do not make a good liar. I have seen that look in your eyes. You are right to say God is enough, but there are few He calls to journey this life alone."

Amos reached back into his scrip and brought out some stale bread. Giving thanks to God, he broke it and gave half to Hosea. Choking down a dry mouthful,

Amos continued, "I think you should consider marriage, Hosea. But I would be of no help in choosing a mate. I would be apt to choose anyone with an ability to cook." Amos made a face as he bit off another piece of the stale loaf.

"Well, if I must be honest," Hosea answered with a shy smile, "and since I can keep nothing from one so wise, I have already made my choice—*if* the Lord calls me to wed."

Amos leaned forward, his eyes reflecting the flames' dance. "Can this be true? Who is she? Do I know her? What tribe is she from?"

"No, no, you do not understand, Amos," Hosea shook his head. "She has no name."

"What do you mean by this? I hope you are ashamed for deceiving an old man."

"I'm sorry, Amos." Hosea laughed. "It's just that the vision of her is so clear in my heart I forget she is one I have never met." Hosea's eyes shone as he continued. "But she will be as sweet as the honeycomb, pure in heart, and will adore children. She will be so meek that lambs are envious, so graceful that gazelles wonder at her, and of course, devoted to the Lord God."

"But will she be able to weave and spin, with arms strong to grind flour for bread?" Amos teased.

"In truth, Amos, I have not considered such things as you mention. I only desire her to love me as much as I already love her."

"And I suppose her left earlobe will hang even with her right, and she will have teeth of pearls, skin as smooth as a fawn, and her garments will sway gently as she walks. Am I right?" Amos laughed when Hosea reddened. "Well, my son, *if* you find such perfection, what makes you believe that she will desire *you*?"

Hosea seemed oblivious to Amos' teasing. "I don't care if she is perfect in outward beauty, only beauty as the Lord sees it. What good is beauty when it has faded? My desire is for a woman who will cherish our life together. Do I ask too much?"

Amos chuckled. "Only a moment ago God was enough for you." They laughed together. Amos blinked and sighed contentedly, then bitterness graveled his voice. "My friend, how will you find this dream to marry? Are there Israelites left that yet adhere to faithfulness and morality? Marriage has crumbled under the weight of sin, and righteousness is but a memory in Israel. Find a wife if you can, but you may have to settle for a little imperfection."

Hosea sobered also. "Maybe the true danger to our country is not foreign powers, but our unfaithfulness to ourselves and to the Lord." He leaned his back against the trunk of an olive tree. "Perhaps I am foolish, Amos. Sometimes I think that if God would create a bride for Himself He could do no better than the one I have imagined. But, of course, who could be equally yoked with El Shaddai?" Hosea sat silent for a moment then looked at Amos and smiled. "Why do you let me ramble on so?"

Amos shrugged and yawned. "It is my only entertainment."

They absently stoked the fire. When Hosea's eyes fluttered in exhaustion, Amos tapped him on the shoulder, suggesting he make his bed in the booth. Hosea gratefully accepted the offer and was soon enjoying a deep, peaceful slumber.

Suddenly he was wide awake. He was not sure why, but he knew he could sleep no longer. Disoriented, he left the booth and surveyed the camp. The minute light of the stars revealed Amos asleep beside the campfire's cold pit.

Hosea was chilled and pulled on his outer tunic. He glanced up at the clear night sky before dawn could obliterate the vision of stars dancing overhead. *How beautiful is your creation, Lord God,* he thought. Somehow he felt the Lord answered him. In a voice barely audible, he thought he heard his name.

His eyes widened in wonder and he checked the sleeping form of Amos. The wind stirred about him and he heard the call again.

"Hosea."

The stars brightened overhead. The Pleiades seemed to sparkle a celestial dance ordained by God. Hosea did not understand. *Is it true? Do the morning stars truly sing together?*

"HOSEA."

The wind carried the sound past him and rippled his cloak. Then it stilled.

"El Shaddai?" Hosea called cautiously. "I am listening."

The long-awaited message of the Lord came sure and quick: "Go and marry a girl who is a prostitute, so that some of her children will be born to you from other men. This will illustrate the way my people have been untrue to me, committing open adultery against me by worshiping other gods."

Hosea stood in awe at the words of the Lord. *Lord, what are you saying? Surely you can't mean it!* There was no answer, but there was finality in the silence. The morning stars faded with the rising of the sun.

"Don't leave me," Hosea whispered. Even as he formed the words he knew the Lord God had not. Once more he felt the presence of the Lord and the peace it brought, although it was contrasted with his horror at taking a harlot to wife.

Why would God consign him to living with a sinful woman? How would her harlotry be a sign to Israel? Didn't his life mean more than a symbol? What about the woman he wanted? He did not want to abandon his visionary bride. How could he love one so different from her?

Hosea wandered absently from the lodge. Sitting cross-legged by the road, he thought hard on what the Lord had spoken. He knew he had received the word of the Lord, but God's purpose was abstract to him.

A camel bearing one lone rider galloped into view, interrupting his thoughts. He quickly rose, his habit of hospitality taking over. "Hail, friend!" Hosea greeted. "Stop and join us for our repast. We have parched grain and dates to share. My friend and I are staying in a lodge just a short distance through those olive trees. Come."

The man slowed his camel but shook his head. His eyes were shadowy and his face filled with grief. "Forgive me, but my venture allows me no time for rest or salutations."

"Is something wrong? Are you in danger?"

The man's lower jaw tensed and he gripped the reigns tightly, halting his beast. "I am in no danger, but . . ." He seemed to be losing composure. Hosea waited as he took a deep breath. "I have come from a city of refuge, Ramoth in Gilead. I went to pay homage in Beth-el for my release. The death of the high priest purchased my freedom. But . . ." the man choked. Hosea felt helpless as he continued in broken sentences. "My family, they live in Tappuah . . . all destroyed."

Hosea's eyes held horror. He questioned the man no further but waited for him to continue the painful report.

"Our new king, Menahem!" He spit the name from his mouth as though it were poison.

"What? Menahem is king?" Hosea echoed blankly.

"Yes. He slew Shallum, then declared himself king. But the people of Tappuah would not accept him, so he *murdered* them!"

"The entire city?"

"He destroyed them all." The man's eyes suddenly clouded with a calculated hatred, and he continued in a voice that made Hosea weep. "Let him return to his throne and boast of his evil with the noise of a dog. His way will be dark and slippery, and he will be hounded forever by the Lord's angel."

"My friend." Hosea moved nearer to touch the hem of the man's garment in sympathy and felt a chill run through him. "You are weary."

As though Hosea were not present, the man continued his bitter cursing while an inhuman smile played about his lips. "O, I plead that the Lord may not consume him, nor the people forget how he shamed them and made them bow before him."

The man trembled with rage, and his wrath consumed him. "I spit upon the eldest son of his loins. May the Lord set corruption upon his head. Because we were made a byword of shame and our children were ripped from their mother's wombs and slain as sheep appointed for meat, may his son be clothed with shame also. Let him be covered with confusion as with a mantle. May sudden destruction come upon him while he is unaware and his carcass be food for the foxes."

His body convulsed once more, then he looked with question at Hosea as though just remembering he was not alone. Giving voice to his passion had momentarily stunned him. "I cannot wait. My purpose will sustain me the rest of the journey. Farewell."

"I understand," Hosea said, but it was doubtful if the

stranger heard him, for he had goaded his camel sharply. He pushed it to the limit of its endurance and attempted to goad it yet further. Soon Hosea lost sight of him.

Hosea darted swiftly back to Amos at the campsite. The prophet had not stirred. Hosea shook him vigorously. "Amos, wake up. I have much to tell you!"

12

*D*on't be like Israel, stubborn as a heifer, resisting the
Lord's attempts to lead her in green pastures.

Hosea 4:16

Hosea shielded his eyes with his hands but the images
his mind had created were engraved forever. Visions of a
typical day in Tappuah haunted him as he traveled. The
streets were filled with laughing children, neighbors calling from rooftops, women chattering at the village well,
and dogs scrounging in the alleys for food.

But sudden darkness devoured the contented scene.
Violence and blood splattered the streets. Only silence
survived Menahem's massacre. A nightmare of mangled
dogs, blood-flooded rooftops, children lying broken in
pools of blood, and bellies of the once-pregnant women
drained of life all swam in Hosea's head. By trampling
Tappuah under his feet Menahem had brought Israel
under his reign of fear, tracking footprints of blood
across an entire nation.

Hosea had gone to Tappuah. Nothing could have prevented his attempt to aid his countrymen, but he had arrived three days after the massacre, and there was noth-

ing left to do. Though the horror of the crime had been scrubbed away by people from neighboring villages, that did not prevent him from visualizing what must have occurred. For Hosea, the horror of the crime would always torment his heart because he knew one day the vision would encompass all Israel.

It was a senseless crime for which there was no remedy. Hosea wanted so badly to help, but he knew there was nothing he could do. The feeling of helplessness overwhelmed him. Maybe he could not erase the tragedy of Tappuah, but he could go home and carry out the directions God had given him. It was Israel's only hope.

The countryside blurred as he plodded over familiar back roads, trusting the way home to his feet. As he approached Samaria a shout startled him. He quickly recognized his brother. Arioch, a younger, more reserved, less rugged version of himself, headed toward him.

"Arioch, my brother! How I have longed to see you." Hosea slapped his brother on the back as they embraced. "How is Lois?"

"She is assisting Bilhah with preparations for your refreshment," Arioch said as he returned his hug. "I saw you a distance from the vineyard and told her of your arrival before I came out to meet you."

"She would have had you stoned had you not given her ample warning." Hosea laughed for the first time since leaving Amos. His feelings for his family warmed him. "Well, Arioch," Hosea laid his arm across his brother's shoulder as they crossed the vineyard toward the city gates. "What of the five years between us? Tell me, are you married? Is Lois?"

Arioch's smile was a little sour. "I spend nearly every hour in the vineyard and olive grove. The rest of my time is spent watching over our little sister, who I have come to believe has no intention of ever marrying. She is content to be mistress of the household and rule our servant, Bilhah. And when I am home she tries to rule me!"

"Well I know, Arioch, well I know." Hosea smiled, remembering his potent little sister, and patted his brother's shoulder in mock sympathy. "Many times while I was away, I envisioned you and Lois sitting in silence that was broken only by threats to slit one another's throat. If I did not know better I would swear you were born of different wombs," Hosea chided.

"You were always the one to handle Lois," Arioch admitted. "Since you left, there has been only strife between us. She refuses to wed, fearful that the house will deteriorate and starvation claim us. She takes much pride in caring for me and I don't like to be taken care of."

"If you have explained this to her, perhaps you should try a different manner," Hosea teased him. "Perhaps a little tact." When Arioch did not laugh, Hosea changed the subject. "How is the property faring?"

"There is constant work just to maintain it. The vines are bent, ready to harvest, while the olives are bursting with readiness too. The vineyard, alone, was meant to be farmed by more than one man, but the two crops together are . . . It is good we have no sheep," Arioch smirked. "Please do not think me bitter for having tended the land alone. It has been pleasant enough, but there is little time for anything else."

Hosea questioned with eyes that saw deeper than words. "I perceive you would have preferred some time to pursue a wife rather than pursuing foxes from the vines."

"I would, if there were prospects. But there have been none."

Hosea smiled. "Now that I am home, there will be some changes made." He chuckled to himself wryly, thinking of the wife he would add to the family. *Many changes.*

Hosea was relieved to see their stone home had not changed since the time his mother had ruled there. Lois obviously ruled now. Hosea and Arioch passed the stairs leading to the roof on the right, and Hosea reveled in the cool, familiar cobblestones of the floor as they entered the huge courtyard. Dominating the center of the court was a perpetually smoking fireplace next to a small cistern, surrounded by storage vessels, cooking pots, baskets, bowls, and serving utensils meticulously arranged according to size. A low table strewn with pottery shard and pruning tools, the only spot in the house where there was a thing out of place, was Arioch's work bench. Three-legged stools were lined up against the long wall beside the fireplace. Hosea fondly recalled the days when their father worked there. The opposite wall held a daybed reserved for guests. That was new since he left. It was spread with a striped carpet and three stuffed cushions of woven goathair.

Hosea saw Lois in the adjoining storage bin before she detected his presence. Her back was to him and she was elbow-deep in flour. The temptation to tease her reawakened in him, and an adolescent grin covered his face. "So this is how a weary traveler is welcomed into the house of our honorable father, Beeri!" He pretended offense.

"Hosea!" Lois's usually sober countenance brightened as she turned, and her flour-dusted arms were about his neck before he could continue. For the moment she was unconcerned about her disheveled state and squealed with delight as Hosea swung her around the room. Arioch beamed. Lois indulged in the frolicking only a moment before pushing herself away to straighten her tunic.

"You deserve a sound thrashing, Brother. How could you have stayed away so long, roaming the mountains like a thief? How is our friend Amos? Why is he not with you?"

"For a moment I was not sure I was home, but now I know of a certainty," Hosea elbowed Arioch and jeered. "You certainly are my own sister, the only woman I know who can love and rebuke without stopping to catch her breath."

Lois laid her hands on her hips and shook her head. "Leave me be now, or I will never finish with your refreshment."

"You are all the refreshment I need, dear sister." Hosea leaned to kiss her cheek and was amused when she ducked, shaking a floured finger in threat. It was good to be home.

The evening hummed with the mercifully monotonous sound of Arioch reviewing the family's financial situation for Hosea. When Hosea laid his head to rest that night he was at peace. He slept soundly for the first time since he visited Tappuah.

"Lois, Arioch, please let your chores wait this morning. I need to speak with you."

Exchanging a confused look with Arioch, Lois asked, "Is there a problem?" Arioch's brow was furrowed also.

"Not exactly." Hosea nervously slapped the back of his hand against the palm of the other.

"You have not taken sick, have you?" Lois reached for his face.

"No." Hosea shrank from her touch. Arioch laid a friendly hand of restraint on Lois's arm. She was twitching with impatience. Hosea turned away to organize his thoughts. Where should he start? Only a week ago he and his old friend had bade each other farewell, and already he longed for Amos' guidance. God had answered all his questions; now he must answer theirs.

"Amos has left for his native Judah," Hosea said and faced them again. "He is no longer the Lord God's prophet to Israel."

"*Oy vey!*" Lois gasped. "Has God left Israel without a prophet?"

"No," Hosea spoke plainly, letting the importance of the words speak for themselves. "He has left Israel with *me*. Before we departed, Amos anointed me with a vial of oil. In truth, the responsibility overwhelms me."

Lois started to speak, but Arioch cautioned her. "Let Hosea continue."

"Like an unbreakable oath, he used my own words to bless me. If I recall rightly, he said I would experience lack as a prophet and I would surely fall short, but I should always remember my own words. That God is called El Shaddai. He is enough."

Lois could no longer keep silent. "But that sounds more like a warning than a blessing."

Hosea nodded. "The words were comforting then, but now they seem foreboding."

"What are you trying to tell us?" Arioch asked.

Hosea covered his face with his hands and prayed silently in desperation. *El Shaddai, how shall I make them understand?* His forehead crinkled, then relaxed into a knowing smile. He dropped his hands, casting his eyes down helplessly. "It is so difficult," he sighed dramatically. "If only there was someone who could help me."

"Hosea," Lois jumped up from the stool and rushed to lay her head on his chest. "Just tell me what I can do."

"You would only think me foolish." Hosea turned his head to the side woefully.

"Please let me help, Hosea," Lois besought him. "I'll do anything for you." Arioch nodded his agreement.

"Very well." Hosea drew in his breath. He had them where he wanted them. "Answer this riddle. When a man enters into a marriage covenant with a woman, and she later falls into adultery, does the man have just cause for handing her a bill of divorcement?"

Arioch looked with question at his brother. "That is no riddle. The law is clear. He may divorce her."

"Ah," Hosea's eyes twinkled. "But where is the mercy, love, and sacrifice he pledged to her?"

"That is foolishness, Hosea," Lois jerked her head. "When a woman deserts her husband, she breaks the covenant and the marriage counts for nothing. Divorcement is the punishment for unfaithfulness."

"Then we are doomed," Hosea spoke quietly. "For God has said the man is the Lord and Israel is the harlot bride."

Lois's mouth flapped. Arioch stared in shock.

"How many times has Israel broken her covenant with the Lord?" Hosea asked sharply.

Arioch and Lois looked at each other. "Well?" Hosea insisted. They were silent. "Answer another riddle," he pressed the point. "If a man loves a woman who is a prostitute, should he marry her?"

"Of course not," Lois sniffed disdainfully. "God commands men to stay far from the evil woman."

"Are you saying that the Lord is breaking His own law by His marriage to the harlot Israel?" Hosea asked. "Can you deny that Israel has been unfaithful to her God?"

Arioch spoke up. "What is the point of this?"

"That there is no mercy in the law, only in love." Hosea's eyes pleaded for them to understand. "El Shaddai has spoken to me. I intend to fulfill his commandment to illustrate His love as the law never will." Hosea looked evenly at his brother and sister. Leaning toward them he took a deep breath and winked. "Do you know of a worthy harlot that I may take to wife?"

Searching the crowded Samaritan streets, Hosea had reason to question his sanity. His earlier vision of a flawless bride chimed its unplayed melody in his mind to mock him. He was not destined to marry his dream. He was never to know love with a meek, virginal maiden. His heart still ached for the one who was to be forever forbidden him. With every step toward the fulfillment of the Lord's desire and the death of his own, the pain of denial grew.

When the crowd and the noise and the stench overwhelmed him Hosea knew he was nearing the marketplace, the most decadent district of Samaria. Having been raised in the city, he knew well why it is said, "If a Samaritan kiss you, count your teeth." He stayed away from open doorways and inventoried himself when he was bumped into.

The corruption sickened him. Every vile allurement created by man was assembled, swarming with flies or covered with excrement and on public display. Hosea was nauseated. *This is no place to find a bride,* he thought.

He was about to turn back when he glanced into an alleyway between two buildings. A thinly layered piece of fabric hanging from a vender's cart obscured his view, but his curiosity held him when his eyes fell on a familiar feminine form. The gauze-like fabric lent an ethereal quality to the young woman's face. He watched the first moments of sunset flitter about her as a dancing butterfly adorning a flower. Her gold and ivory ornaments, bright dress, and bold mannerisms belied his earlier angelic impression. Still, Hosea was enraptured with the innocence he thought he saw, just as he had been two years ago in another marketplace in Beth-el, when the girl was the new bride of the high priest.

He was shocked to see her reach for a man and press herself to him. Even at a distance he caught the mischievous flicker dancing in the black wilderness of her eyes, highlighting the sensuous curve of her lips as she smiled. Her belled ankle bracelet jingled as she stomped her foot and tossed her head, shaking her dark, waist-length curls in a fit of laughter.

Hosea saw the two whisper together. She threw her arms around him and boldly kissed him on the mouth. As they kissed she jiggled a satchel of gold hanging by a rope tied around the man's waist. She smiled seductively. The man fondled her, then left.

The prophecy! Hosea had nearly forgotten it. *She is a harlot, fulfilling the prophecy Amos gave Amaziah long ago in Beth-el.* He remembered how he had compared her to stiff-necked Israel, and he knew she was the one God had chosen for him.

He cringed. Suddenly his visionary bride loomed invitingly between him and his harlot wife. Her form grew into a colossal image, blocking out all else. Then the brightness of her purity faded. The apparition darkened, contorting itself. Hosea watched his virginal dream decay and crystalize into a black, molten Baal.

I see now, Lord, Hosea marveled at the revelation. *I thought I served only You, but a dream has captured my heart also—a dream that prevented my full surrender to You. Forgive me.*

The vision shattered, and Hosea's eyes focused once again on Gomer. This was the one God intended for him, and she would have to be enough to fulfill his expectations. As he gently pulled aside the linen garment of the vender's cart, the brashness in her features was evident, but Hosea chose to impress forever in his memory the delicate vision of her he had beheld through the veil.

Now, how shall I win her? Hosea thought, and suddenly he felt challenged. He chuckled. *I wonder if the Lord feels such a challenge with His harlot Israel?* He entered the alleyway, approaching her. She scrutinized him, but no recognition was present in her expression. *I am just another prospective customer to her!* Hosea thought with disgust, but his chagrin left as they stood close enough to touch. She smiled coyly. Though her indiscreet clothing and the reek of too much perfume attempted to bury her beauty, it failed. *She is still lovely,* Hosea thought.

With hands on her hips she held her head askance and questioned him. "My name is Gomer, how may I help you?"

"You don't remember me, do you?"

Gomer winked at him suggestively. "Is there any reason I should?"

Embarrassed, Hosea looked down and shuffled his feet.

"By the gods!" Her voice enlivened when she recognized Hosea's tall frame. "I do remember you. You were the prophet's companion at the marketplace in Beth-el. What brings you to me?" Gomer mistook his silence, and a twinge of bitterness laced her tone as she spoke. "So, a man of God has desires as other men. I don't know why I should have thought differently." She crossed her arms in a businesslike manner. "What will you give me if I let you come in?" She jerked her head toward a door behind her.

"No, Gomer," Hosea protested. "You do not understand." He looked dismayed and shifted his weight. "I . . . I . . . want you to be my wife."

"Are you drunk?" Gomer narrowed her eyes at him.

"I'm as sober and as serious as I've ever been in my life," Hosea proclaimed, and found himself truly wanting Gomer to accept his offer.

"If this is some new game, I'm not amused." Gomer stomped her foot in anger, certain she was being misled in jest. "Do not waste my time with foolishness. Hurry now, prophet, before your God finds you with a harlot."

"But you do not understand. God sent me—"

"Look, prophet, do you see the king's horse tethered to that cart and the soldiers beside it? If you do not leave this moment I will call for them and—"

"Gomer, please, you—" Hosea cut himself off and stepped back. "If this is your will, I will go." He bowed politely.

She turned her back on him, a sign she meant for him to go. Hosea left, saddened by her rejection but not hopeless. He was certain Gomer was God's choice for him and wondered how God was going to break her stubborn resistance. *Maybe, if I tried again in a different . . .* He turned back, but she was gone.

He heard a scuffle coming from the other side of the street, and saw Gomer struggling with the soldiers she had just proposed as her rescuers. Dragging her against her will, they forced her into a horsedrawn cart.

Hosea shouted to the soldiers over the shrill threats of Gomer, but they ignored him. He reached the cart just as they drove away. Hosea grabbed at the soldier holding

Gomer, but the cart jolted, hurtling him to the ground. Stunned from the fall, Hosea chased after them with difficulty. The cart sped up the narrow street, quickly climbing the spiral turns toward the palace, jostling out of Hosea's sight.

With long-legged strides, Hosea covered the distance hastily. Outside the palace grounds, he hid himself among a crowd of boisterous citizens eager to be entertained with Gomer's struggle against the soldiers. Unable to follow her into the palace, Hosea was forced to wait at a spiked iron gate. Helplessly he watched Gomer being crudely corralled through the palace doors. He realized with a bit of shock that his knuckles were white with anger as they gripped the bars of the gate.

Inside the palace, away from the jeers of the crowd, Gomer quieted as she was led to the throne room. She cleared her throat and glanced quickly about the huge hall. In contrast to the many spectators in the room, there were few furnishings. A lavish throne, overspread with hind pelts, rose threateningly at the head of the hall. The tiled floor and high, sculptured ceiling echoed the low murmur of the crowd.

Once more she stood before Menahem, only now he was king and had guards gripping her arms as reinforcements of his power. She was not too distracted to notice that kingship had changed Menahem little. *He still wears pride like a suit of armor. I am awed by him more each time I see him*, she thought. She felt the familiar resistance rising in her. She knew she must express respect, however; he held too much power for her to speak her mind.

With arms behind his back and a cocky smile, Menahem descended from his throne and paced around his captive, thoroughly inspecting her. "Gomer, how good it is to see you once more. I trust you have not driven yourself mad with loneliness and grief since your beloved husband, the high priest, died."

Her eyes narrowed, but she held her tongue. She struggled under the grip of the soldiers, and with a nod from Menahem they freed her.

"Your silence has me baffled, woman. But a few years ago, you would have stabbed at me with your insolent words. What has changed?"

"If the fox is king, bow before him."

Menahem smiled pompously. "Indeed." He stroked her cheek with the back of his hand. "Then you are afraid of me now?"

"No."

The king walked behind her and toyed with the ends of her hair. "That is good. For I would not want a mare of my stable frightened into passivity."

"What do you mean, 'a mare of my stable'?" Gomer was wary.

"I mean, little Gomer, that I have appropriated to myself all the former wives of Amaziah." He twirled one of her black curls between his finger and thumb. "And I have all of them but one."

No! Gomer thought, but dared not cry aloud. *Never! I will die before I become a concubine again.* Desperately, hopelessly, she sought some form of escape. Her eyes darted to the window where freedom awaited, and she caught a glimpse of Hosea, still clutching the gate. An idea formed.

"When I became king, I had hoped you would seek my favor," Menahem whispered in her ear while he caressed her neck and shoulders. "But when you did not come, I began to think what sport hunting a wild mare could be. So I began the chase."

137

"You will not throw a harness around my neck, sire."

"Ah," his eyes gleamed. "Already you begin the game."

"You do not understand. I cannot become your wife."

Menahem turned her about and stared coldly. He placed his arms behind his back once more and paced before her. "No, it is you who do not understand. You have been brought before this court on charges of prostitution. You may plead guilty, harlot," his voice boomed, "and suffer at the hands of my executioners. Or you may enter the court as my concubine. Those are the choices."

Gomer stared straight ahead. "I am obligated to another."

"What?" Menahem's eyes bulged.

Gomer pointed out the window to Hosea. "I am betrothed to Hosea, the prophet of the Lord."

13

So Hosea married Gomer, daughter of Diblaim.

Hosea 1:3

Gomer and Hosea left the palace together. They walked in silence toward her home at the edge of the marketplace. Gomer finally spoke. "If you had not been at the palace gates, my situation would be quite distressing now."

"If that is gratitude, you are most welcome," Hosea said and stopped to bow in the middle of the narrow city street. Gomer played along with a curtsy, for his behavior was reminiscent of Ka'Tan's. A sudden change in Hosea's demeanor arrested her attention.

"I know we have only just met," he said shyly, his eyes on the ground, "but I've already proposed to you, and . . . well, I . . ."

Gomer laughed. "Are you still trying to find out my price?"

Hosea shook his head vehemently. "No, not at all. There is . . . there is something I must know." He cleared his throat before going on. "Is escape from the king's harem the only reason you accepted my proposal?" He was surprised the thought mattered so much to him. He had been worried he would not have affection for a harlot spouse. It never occurred to him that she would not care for him.

"Why else?" Gomer answered in a jocular manner, but she was immediately sorry when Hosea looked dejectedly at the ground. He kicked gently at a shard of broken pottery in the road, reminding Gomer of a pouting boy. Her expression became apologetic. "I guess that makes you my hero."

"I suppose it does," Hosea said absently. Stopping again he looked at her seriously. "My proposal was in earnest. Was your acceptance?"

"Do you mean, am I really going to marry you?"

Hosea looked at her expectantly with his large, unblinking sheep eyes. *Those eyes!* Gomer thought, scanning the transparency of their emerald borders. *He could never deceive anyone; not with eyes that give away his every thought.*

Gomer looked away from Hosea toward the palace. *Indeed, I have little choice. If I choose not to marry him, I will have to hide from the king, and I cannot live that way. I could move to another city, but if I do, I'll lose the slim hope of finding Dan. Menahem is a stubborn mule,* Gomer tapped her foot as she mulled. *He will not leave me in peace if I do not marry Hosea. It seems he has made the choice for me.* Gomer felt frustrated that someone was interfering in her life again. *Still,* she looked back at Hosea, *marriage to him would not be the worst that I have endured from life.*

The steady flow of people surging through the streets jostled the couple so badly they had a hard time standing still. But the determination in Hosea's stance said he would not move until Gomer had answered him.

"I think I should complete what you have begun."
Gomer laughed. "But I give you fair warning, you may
not be prepared for the trials that await such an uncommon pair as we shall make."

"I may be more able than you think." Hosea grinned
widely, creating delightful crinkles around his eyes. "I
wonder if *you* are as capable as you expect me to be?"

"I do not claim *your* competence, good sir, only foresight," Gomer teased, and then added with a slight wrinkle to her brow, "Surely you cannot think it an easy
thing to marry a . . . such a one as I."

"I have not requested ease from the Lord. I live by the
principles of love and justice and always expect much
from God."

Gomer lifted her chin in mirth. "If you are bent on this
marriage, I promise you will be getting much, *much*
more than you expect!"

"And you, Gomer?" Hosea asked. "What guides your
life?"

"I too live by the principles of love," Gomer smirked
sarcastically, but this time Hosea's face remained somber. "I do what I must to live," she muttered.

"Have you no family to care for you?"

"Only a brother. I came to Samaria two years ago to
find him. When I couldn't, I had to survive, so. . . ." She
left the sentence hanging.

Hosea reached for Gomer's hand and squeezed it. "I
am truly sorry." He seemed to be apologizing for all the
sadness in her life. The sincerity of his tone was convincing. Gomer could almost believe he really cared for her.

He went on, "I am looking forward to our betrothal. A
year seems so little time to learn all I wish to know about
you."

Gomer did not try to suppress her throaty laughter.

She threw back her head and roared. "I hope it does not take you *that* long."

"What do you mean?" Hosea was obviously startled by her jarring laugh.

Gomer patted her midsection daintily, an incongruous contrast with the boisterous noise she made. "I am with child." Her eyes twinkled mischievously.

Hosea suspected she thought this would change his mind. *Well, the Lord God said some of her children would be born to me from other men.* Setting his chin, he touched her elbow to steer toward her house again. "Gather your things. I will come for you at sunset tomorrow."

"Then you still want to—"

"Marry you?" he smiled. "I too like to complete what has begun."

Gomer nodded her approval. She studied Hosea's profile as they walked, noting how much of his attractiveness did not come from physical appearance. Again, as in Beth-el, she was drawn to him, though the man was a riddle. The ridiculous circumstances of their acquaintance notwithstanding, she thought she could grow to like Hosea.

At her door Gomer seemed to realize for the first time that they had been holding hands, and she jerked her hand free. Hosea was stunned. Searching her face, he sought the reason for the mysterious longing that seemed to sketch her features but found only the barrier she erected. She was a paradox, craving love yet resisting it. He firmly took her hand and bent to kiss it. A surprising innocence surfaced with her blush that stemmed from more than tender age. *She is so beautiful,* he repeated to himself yet again.

"Why do you stare?" Gomer resumed her composure, irritated at herself for blushing.

"I am awed by your beauty."

Gomer was surprised that a prophet would admire anything about a harlot. "It is going to take me some time to grow accustomed to you."

"Then I'm glad you'll be starting tomorrow."

Gomer had no witty response. It seemed this man never said what one would expect. She turned to enter her room.

"May I come in with you?" Hosea's words stopped her cold. Gomer's look pierced him. How many times she had heard those words. Was Hosea no different after all? *Please*, she silently pleaded, *don't disappoint me. Don't turn out to be like all the others.*

Hosea seemed to read her thoughts. He quickly added, "Do you have wine? We are not lawfully betrothed yet, and I wish to drink the cup of the covenant with you."

"Oh," was all Gomer could manage. Once inside her dreary apartment, darkened with wooden idols, Gomer produced a gourd filled with spiced pomegranate wine and two goblets. Hosea poured solemnly, and then handing her a cup, faced her. His eyes looked deep into hers.

"Since you have no earthly father, I make my contract for you with the Father in heaven. With Him as my witness I vow to care for you tenderly all the days of your life, and to provide for you and our children." Hosea emphasized the word "our" as his eyes darted to Gomer's stomach.

An involuntary shiver was Gomer's response to his words. Hosea continued. "Though the dwelling I call home is of substance, it is an inheritance from my deceased parents, to be shared with my brother and sister. I have no earthly possessions of my own to offer for a bride price." Hosea's voice was low and breathy. "So I beseech the Lord God of Israel, and you, to accept my life in payment."

The enchantment of the moment went beyond the business of betrothal. Gomer sensed an eerie spiritual quality that she could not begin to fathom, but full understanding seemed to underscore Hosea's words.

"Do you accept the terms of my proposal?"

So enraptured had Gomer been by Hosea's mystique the thought had not occurred to her that she played any part in this drama. She was startled by his question. What could she say to such an offer? "I accept."

"I am most pleased." Hosea smiled intimately as he intertwined their arms, his eyes never leaving hers. They drank the covenant cup, and Gomer was filled with warmth that came from more than strong wine.

Suddenly Hosea was at the door. "I go to prepare a place for you. Though I must leave you now, I will surely return and bring you to it."

He was gone.

The unseasonal coolness of the summer evening was a blessing. Gomer was packed and waiting to be taken as the wife of Hosea, the prophet. *I am a fool,* she grimaced. *He will not come. What could a man of God want with a wanton woman for a wife? This all must be some vast joke.*

A timid knock interrupted her thoughts. When Gomer opened the door, a strange woman ducked in quickly, as if to hide. "I am Lois, sister of Hosea." The woman's eyes bulged. "I have been sent to assist you in the wedding preparations." Her voice made it clear she was there under protest. She threw disapproving glances quickly about the room, avoiding Gomer.

"What preparations?" Gomer asked coldly. "I am packed and dressed. There is nothing more to do."

Lois looked reproachfully at the gaudy costume of her brother's bride. Her face paled.

Gomer could not resist mocking this priggish woman. "What is wrong?" She feigned distress. "Is my dress soiled?"

"It is no matter." Lois waved her hand with an air of superiority. "I should have expected as much."

Gomer's hands clenched her hips in anger. A loud rapping at the door prevented the brawl that would have surely taken place.

"My joy will not be restrained," Hosea sang merrily at the door for all to hear. "My heart can be kept waiting no longer for the honor of your hand."

Hosea made such a racket that even Gomer was embarrassed. For him to pretend their marriage was honorable behind closed doors was one thing, but did he have to be so dramatic about what was already a public spectacle? Though it was nightfall, his screeching would surely bring out the entire city. Even now she could hear the crowd gathering. They sounded gruesomely eager for her appearance.

Gomer threw open the door. Hosea was on the stoop, grinning widely, and another man, apparently his brother, stood awkwardly behind him. *So this is the extent of the grand procession. A marked difference from my first wedding.* Gomer tossed her head.

The mob behind Hosea was crowding closer, nudging each other in anticipation of Gomer's public disgrace.

Some of the men in the crowd snickered suggestively. Lois hung her head in open humiliation. Gomer was stirred to action. *No one will laugh at me!*

In the manner she had used when surrounded by royalty, she stepped regally to Hosea's side. His dark hair was oiled elegantly, and his cheeks were bright with excitement. He towered above her in sincere joy, a sentiment Gomer found completely inexplicable.

She followed his lead. Holding her head high, she smiled defiantly at the mass of curious onlookers, accentuating the fact that she wore no bridal veil. The pious women in the crowd turned their backs on her, and the men, many of them former customers, leered and scoffed. But from the demeanor of the bride and groom one would have taken the mocking throng to be joyful friends of a highly esteemed couple.

"That's it, my love," Hosea whispered to her. "Don't let them deter us. We have a destiny to fulfill." Gomer's mouth dropped open. His words never ceased to astound her.

14

I don't want your sacrifices—I want your love; I don't want your offerings—I want you to know me.

Hosea 6:6

As the couple entered their rooftop chambers, Hosea stood back to watch Gomer's reaction. The simplistic beauty which greeted her was a pleasant sight. She could only gape. Arranged in the corners and encircling the couch which lined one wall of the room were bundles of myrtle branches, their tiny white flowers budding profusely. They were tied with delicate strips of fine white linen. The floor was strewn with myrtle petals that had been picked one by one from the flowers to release the refreshing scent. The roof swirled with the tingling aroma.

Gomer turned to Hosea, who rested his lengthy limbs against the doorpost. He was positively glowing at her. She fumbled for words. "The nature of our . . ah . . . marriage, led me to . . . I mean, I thought you . . . that is, I did not expect such preparation."

"I know," Hosea said, still beaming at her. "But I kept thinking how El Shaddai is planning such loving preparations for our people, and, well, if He would do that for us, then why shouldn't I for you?"

Gomer covered her cheeks. *Why am I blushing like some silly virgin?* she reprimanded herself. "I give you my thanks," she said stiffly. Try as she might, she could think of nothing else to say. *I was right to think Hosea was uncommon when I first saw him in Beth-el,* she mused. *He treats a harlot like the purest bride.*

Hosea crossed over to a bedcushion nestled on the floor amid the myrtle petals. Easing himself onto it he held out his hand to her. "Come, sit with me."

Hosea's eyes brimmed with love, but Gomer could sense no banal desire in them. *If not for lust, then for what does he beckon me?* She felt awkward. Lust was the only manly emotion she was comfortable with. She sat beside him, wondering what to expect.

Hosea cupped her face in his hands in an unmistakable gesture of desire, yet even as his eyes neared hers in the kiss, she could find no bestial craving lurking there. She was puzzled. Hosea gently laid her back upon the cushion. Her musing quickly ceased as he brushed her forehead with his lips. He smelled of freshly turned earth after a spring rain. She felt cleansed in the very act that usually left her feeling violated.

Suddenly Hosea pulled away, confusing his bride. She searched the darkness for the outline of his face. "Have I displeased you?" Gomer asked in humiliation. She had never displeased a man before.

"It is not that, my love," Hosea's voice was low. "I wondered if it was not I that had displeased you."

"*You* displease *me*?" Gomer exclaimed. Never had she given thought to being pleased by a man. "What do you mean?"

"You are so still. You lie as if waiting for me to be done with you. Am I so distasteful?"

Gomer was amazed to hear him speak of such tender topics. Was he not afraid of sounding unmanly? She could hear the hurt in his voice though, and she answered. "Hosea, you are not distasteful. Would you believe me if I told you that as many men as I have lain with, never before did I find pleasure, until I felt your touch?" She was surprised, even pleased, that she felt this way.

Hosea pulled her head against his chest. "Then why do you not respond to my touch?"

Gomer could say nothing, on the verge of tears that Hosea would care about her feelings. Hosea waited silently for her answer and stroked her hair tenderly. Finally she spoke in a broken voice. "Never has a man requested that *I* find enjoyment with him."

Hosea felt as if his heart would tear. He wanted so much to make Gomer feel loved. He knew he cradled in his arms the body of a mature woman, with the soul of an orphaned child who had never learned how to love. *El Shaddai*, he beseeched, *show me how to love her.*

He embraced Gomer's limp form and rubbed his cheek softly on her hair. "Gomer," he whispered into her ear. "It is not enough for *me* to know you; I want for *you* to know me also."

A sob wrenched itself from somewhere so deeply within Gomer that its source had escaped her notice before. Her arms crept shyly around Hosea's shoulders, and for the first time in her life, rather than simply allowing a man to take her, she gave of herself.

15

My heart cries out within me; how I long to help you! . . . They lie there sleepless with anxiety, but won't ask my help.

Hosea 11:8; 7:14

A long, gutteral groan escaped Gomer's contorted lips. "I can't!" she screamed at Lois.

"You must," Lois's voice was harsh. "Just one more push. After he is born you can ignore him like you have your other two children, but at least bring him into the world safely. Do this one thing for him."

Gomer moaned. "You don't understand. I—" She was cut off as another contraction overtook her. The double-humped seat of the birthing stool was cutting off the circulation in her legs. It seemed her thighs had been propped on it for hours. Her back ached with the effort of straining to a sitting position.

"Gomer!" Lois's voice whipped her ears. "You must stop fighting it. If you don't relax you will damage the baby's head. Let loose and push, no matter how much it hurts."

"You are enjoying my suffering, aren't you?" Gomer panted between contractions.

Outside the door of the little upper room Hosea's brow creased. Painfully he listened to the two women he loved at each other's throats. He pounded his fist in frustration, the emotion most familiar to him lately. For over three years he had withstood Gomer's rejection and given her only love in return, but when the objects of her antipathy included the children it became almost more than he could bear.

Three-year-old Jezreel tugged at his robe. "I thought you were asleep." Hosea tousled his hair

"Baby yet?" Jezreel's expectant eyes shone in the darkness.

"Not yet." Hosea laughed. The boy's unruly brown hair alternately hid, then revealed his soft, brown eyes as he jumped up and down impatiently. Jezreel looked so much like Hosea it was easy to pretend he was the boy's father.

"Abba?" Another voice, much older than its two years, drifted through the night air, seeking permission to come to Hosea.

Hosea squinted and could barely distinguish Loruhamah's form at the bottom of the stairs. She shivered in the cold of the courtyard, where the fire had been neglected in favor of the travailing in the upper room.

"Come, daughter," Hosea said in a gentle voice, and the child darted up the stairs into his arms. As he bounced her on his hip he looked into the dark, brooding eyes that were so much like Gomer's. Studying them, he worried about her aloofness, evident from birth. Even after being prematurely weaned from her mother's breast when Gomer refused to nurse any longer, Loruhamah had coped with little sign of a struggle.

Once more Hosea tried to determine what had caused Gomer to become so cold toward him and the children after their daughter's birth. He searched his memory, hoping to fathom what had turned her from them. His heart lurched when a constricted scream returned him to the present.

"A son!" Lois shouted. "A son is born!"

She holds him as if he were her own, Gomer thought bitterly of her sister-in-law, falling back in exhausted relief. *I wish he were.*

Hosea bounded into the room like a clumsy bear cub, his face alight with the joy of a new son. He knelt beside Gomer and tried to kiss her forehead, but she held him back with her hand.

"Did you find a woman to nurse him, Hosea?"

He swallowed hard. "I hoped you would change your mind."

"Hosea," was all she said, but her tone reinforced her decision. She turned away from him.

Hosea watched as Lois rubbed the baby down with salt and bound him in swaddling cloth, his face reflecting his confusion. Lois caught his eye and shrugged her shoulders, indicating she thought Gomer was hopeless. Hosea ignored her.

He reached for his son when Lois was finished. Her cooing and the warmth of the blankets had soothed the newborn, and his screaming lessened. Hosea brought him to Gomer's side for inspection. "Gomer, look how handsome he is. He has your dark, curly hair and strong forehead."

"Stop it, Hosea. Take him from me," Gomer shrieked, her feeble voice straining till it cracked.

Hosea withdrew with the baby. His tolerance was fading, but he spoke sympathetically. "You're weak now. Maybe later, when you have rested." He stood to leave.

Gomer jerked her head back toward him. "His howling torments me," she explained apologetically, biting her lip when the suffering in Hosea's eyes assaulted her.

"I know, Gomer. I know," he nodded, but he didn't know. *How can any woman reject her own children?* he wondered. He walked to the door.

"Hosea," Gomer's voice was filled with the fear that had marked her demeanor since Lo-ruhamah's birth. "Don't leave me alone. Will you sit beside me until I fall asleep?"

Hosea glanced at the door where Jezreel and Lo-ruhamah peered in, their faces beaming at the baby in his arms. With his back still to her he asked, "May the children come in, too?"

Gomer hesitated. "Yes," she sighed.

After showing them how to safely cuddle their new brother, Hosea hushed the children and they quickly fell asleep at his feet. Lois came in to tell Hosea the woman who would nurse the baby was downstairs, and she took the fussing newborn to his nourishment.

When Hosea looked back at Gomer she was staring at him. "Are you going to call him by some odd name like you did the other two?"

"His name is Lo-ammi," Hosea answered. "The Lord said to name him "Not Mine" for Israel is not His any longer."

Gomer did not answer. Soon Hosea's back relaxed against the wall and his head nodded in slumber. *If only I could rest, too.* Gomer stared at the ceiling. She looked lovingly at Jezreel and Lo-ruhamah. Her arms ached to pull them to her breast, but she restrained herself, as she always did. She must. When Lo-ruhamah was born she found herself overcome with motherly affections.

She started having terrifying nightmares about one of the children dying. During the dreams a voice repeated a vow of vengeance over and over, again and again. The words sounded familiar, but Gomer could not remember where she had heard them. She thought the Lord was threatening to make her pay for her immorality. Night after night she awoke drenched with her own sweat. The grief that pummeled her in the dreams was a grueling revival of the agony of her father's death. Gomer clenched her fist. *I cannot let that happen to me again. I can't bear it!* She slammed the fist down on her mat.

Gomer looked at Hosea, slumped against the wall. *His love is so comforting*—a tear slid from her eye—*but it is not satisfying. I long for something that's, that's . . .* She sighed deeply as her eyelids fluttered and sleep finally put her troubled thoughts to rest.

16

Oh, how can I give you up, my Ephraim? How can I let you go? . . . I did not come to destroy.

Hosea 11:8–9

Bilhah peered around the corner and cautiously looked into the courtyard. She was greeted by flying dust from Gomer's frenzied broom. The servant was stealing away when a sneeze revealed her presence.

"Bilhah!" Gomer's voice cracked like a sling, and the servant reluctantly appeared to help her new mistress rearrange the pandemonium that had set in since Lois's departure two Sabbaths past. When Lois received word of her cousin Lydia's illness she left the household to Gomer, and with a doubtful frown, departed quickly. But the day of Passover preparation was at hand, and Lois was due to return. Gomer had taken no notice of household tasks before. Attempting them with only Bilhah's addled instructions proved to be quite a challenge, but she was determined to prevail.

Gomer shoved the broom at the servant. "Finish this sweeping while I feed the children. The house is in upheaval from searching for the Passover dishes, and still they are nowhere to be found. The men will be coming in from the fields soon, and I must prepare their food. Before you sweep, Bilhah, I'll need some figs and parched corn, and—Lo-ammi, no!" Gomer ran to the baby and pulled his hand away from the oven's flames.

"Jezreel, watch your brother and sister while I prepare something for you to eat." She plopped the baby in the four-year-old's lap before he had a chance to object. "Where is Lo-ruhamah?" Gomer asked. She called but there was no answer. "Jezreel, go look for your sister."

Jezreel placed the baby on the floor. Lo-ammi immediately crawled toward the flaming pit.

"No, Lo-ammi!" Gomer screamed and raced for her child. "Jezreel, hold him again. *I'll* look for Lo-ruhamah." She took a deep breath and searched the house. "Where is that child?" she asked herself. "Must I hunt through the entire house to find her? Why do things look so simple when Lois does them?" she mumbled as she searched.

She found her daughter sitting in the flour bin, giggling as she covered herself with flour. "I just swept this floor!" Gomer tried desperately to control her temper. Picking up the child she shook her over the flour bin while Lo-ruhamah giggled harder. "What will your Aunt Lois say?" she admonished. "This is not the usual ground corn or barley that makes our bread, but freshly ground wheat from the plateaus of Beth-arbel. A precious treat. Aunt Lois will have you thrashed," Gomer continued her scolding. "Now, stay with your brother." With a gentle swat she sent her daughter back into the courtyard.

As Gomer cleaned up after Lo-ruhamah she found some dried fig cakes that Lois had left and revoked the curse she had placed on her sister-in-law for having abandoned her. Gomer remembered the taunting laughter of Lois's doubt in her ability to handle the house, and a new determination set in. She would prove her wrong. *If Lois can do it, I surely can do it better.* Besides, it seemed to mean much to Hosea and it felt good to please him for a change. "By the gods, I will do this for him!" she said triumphantly as she brought the cakes into the courtyard and placed them on the meal mat, arranging three pillows for the children to sit upon. Satisfied, she glanced at her children and forced another smile.

Lo-ruhamah laughed mischievously and Lo-ammi swung his arms, hitting Jezreel as he swayed from side to side. Jezreel accepted his little brother's abuse calmly and returned his mother's smile. It was difficult to keep from melting before their charm, so Gomer occupied her thoughts. *Well, it seems taking care of the house is not as impossible as I first believed.* She left to pour the children some water but hurried back at the sound of Lo-ammi's scream. She inspected the baby and found a red mark on his arm. "What did you do to him, Jezreel?"

"Ro-rahmah, Ro-rahmah," Jezreel cried at the unjust accusation, pointing at his sister.

"Can't I accomplish anything without you children interfering?" Gomer tried to remain calm and seated the children on their cushions.

"Milk, Mamma." Lo-ruhamah held out her cup of water.

"Be glad you have the water, child," Gomer snapped. She would not admit her lack of expertise in milking a goat. "Now eat your cakes."

She left the court and knelt before the wooden kneading trough set on the roof, mercilessly pounding out her frustrations on an innocent mass of dough. She made a face when it stuck to her hands. "This will be bread? How am I to bake without leaven?" she questioned the pile of dough oozing between her fingers. Muttering under her breath she descended to the flour bin and grabbed an extra handful of flour to add to the massive ball of dough. She divided it into two smaller balls which she pressed to ready for the flat stones of the oven. She had seen Lois do the same hundreds of times.

Gomer heard the screaming before she entered the courtyard. The children had dumped water on the floor and crumbled cake floated about in it from the game they made of their food. Bilhah must have been distracted by their noise. Gomer watched as she hurried in with the requested figs. The huge basket obstructed her view and Bilhah slipped in a puddle of the spilled water. The figs flew everywhere. Gomer collapsed on the threshold, a ball of dough still cupped in each hand, and wept quietly.

"Gomer! Arioch and I are famished. I—" Hosea's voice trailed off as he entered and surveyed the room.

Gomer lifted a face streaked with dirt, flour, and tears to her husband. She could contain herself no longer. She burst into frustrated sobs, dabbing at her eyes with her tunic, smearing more flour and dough on her face. The children cowered in silence, saturated with their doughy mess. Bilhah scurried quietly on her hands and knees, picking up figs.

Noting Gomer's pitiful expression, Hosea tried to speak some encouraging word, but instead a chuckle escaped his lips. Hearty laughter followed, erupting from him as he shook his head, unable to stop.

Gomer scowled and threw one of the dough balls at him, but she missed and it landed in Arioch's face. Hosea laughed the harder, holding his sides. Gomer squinted, and with careful aim, the last ball hit its mark.

"Abba's dinner?" Jezreel pointed at his father. Gomer

laughed loudly as Hosea scraped the dough from his face. The children relaxed and Bilhah straightened, forgetting the figs. The room exploded in laughter. Hosea grabbed Gomer and swung her around the fire in uproarious mirth. He kissed away the last of her frustration.

"I tried so hard to make everything perfect for you, Hosea."

Hosea smiled. "I know you did, and I'm very pleased. You have filled my heart with singing."

Gomer looked up at him. "But your meal is ruined. What will you eat?"

Hosea glanced at his brother and winked. "At least we shall not eat of the bread of idleness today, shall we, brother?"

Arioch smiled. "No, indeed not. But how long do you think daily entertainment can sustain us?"

"Careful, brother, there may be dough left." Gomer smiled when Hosea pretended to duck a flying ball. He kissed her on the cheek and patted the children, heading for the door. "Have Bilhah bring fruit and water to the field. That should keep us until evening."

Outside, Hosea stopped his brother. "Didn't I tell you she was softening?"

"Yes, Hosea. I can see she is trying hard to please you," Arioch agreed with pleasure in his face.

" 'Hope deferred makes the heart sick, but when dreams come true at last, there is life and joy,' " Hosea quoted the proverb. "I am full of joy, Arioch. Gomer and I shall fulfill my dreams of a wonderful marriage after all. Surely she is close to repentance."

"But be patient about her abilities," Arioch chided. "Judging from the present state of our home, it may take her years to adjust. Do you think she will ever learn to manage alone?"

Hosea could not help but laugh again at his wife's attempt. "If her heart is in it, that is enough for me."

The men separated to work in opposite ends of the vineyard. Hosea snipped absently at the demanding vines, chuckling intermittently when he thought of how childlike Gomer's face looked covered with flour. He did not notice the clouds gathering overhead until the sky was dark and hazy. Hosea looked for Arioch and shouted across the vineyard. "A storm is gathering. Do you think we should go home?"

Arioch seemed to ignore him. Hosea shouted louder, but still Arioch did not look up. He was about to call to Arioch once more when he felt a presence, the same presence he had known the night he had camped at the abandoned lodge with Amos. Quickly he glanced at Arioch, but his brother continued to turn the earth methodically in silence.

This time Hosea did not wait to be called. He scanned the overcast sky and whispered, "El Shaddai?"

Hosea did not hear a voice. Instead, the presence of God filled him and he was flooded with peace. Hosea closed his eyes and smiled, waiting for the Lord's message. Suddenly he dropped his pruning knife and shouted, "No!" The sky cleared as if it had never darkened. "No, El Shaddai! I need more time. Do You not know what this will do to her, to us? No! No!" He pounded his fists into his thighs.

"Hosea, what is it?" Arioch ran to him.

Hosea looked at his brother with darkened eyes. "El Shaddai spoke to me just now. He said it is time for me to preach the love of God to His harlot, Israel."

"Why does that anger you?"

"Don't you see? It means I must tell Israel she has the heart of a harlot. I must use the story of my own wife, my

160

own marriage as an example! All that Gomer has gained toward a change of heart could be destroyed."

Arioch looked at his brother sternly. "Or it could be strengthened. Listen to me, Hosea." Arioch took hold of his brother's shoulders. "Don't you think God knows what He is doing? You claim to be the Lord's prophet and yet you won't trust Him with what is dearest to your heart. Would you refuse to serve your people because you question the outcome in your marriage? Woe to you, Hosea, if you desert Israel in this."

Hosea gaped at Arioch. His brother was right. He must do as God asked, regardless of Gomer's reaction. But wasn't there some way to protect Gomer from the heartbreak? "Of course, there is no questioning El Shaddai. I must obey Him. Arioch, will you go to the house with me?"

Arioch patted his brother on the shoulder reassuringly, and they left the fields. A peal of thunder rumbled as though a reminder of the Lord God's authority and the message from the gray sky. Hosea felt no better than if he had been visited by the Angel of Death.

17

They shall disappear like morning mist, like dew that quickly dries away, like chaff blown by the wind, like a cloud of smoke.

Hosea 13:3

Gomer was pleasantly surprised to see Hosea and Arioch. "What brings you back from the fields so early?" she asked, looking up from her sweeping. Gomer was further dismayed when Arioch herded the children up the stairs to the roof.

"See how tidy I have made it?" she chirped to her silent husband, attempting to draw him into conversation. "When you left I didn't think I would ever be done." Gomer's tone was light, but she eyed Hosea anxiously. The look on his face scared her.

He stood in the center of the storage room where she was working. His eyes emitted unspoken apologies. It was a long time before he spoke, and then his voice was weighted with sorrow. "Gomer," he began slowly. "You know that I have been awaiting the time when El Shaddai would send me out to preach repentance to our idolatrous country."

Gomer nodded. She had never understood Hosea's religious inclinations, but well she knew of them.

"A while ago, in the vineyard, God spoke to me." Hosea trembled. "He said He wanted me to go and tell His people that they have played the harlot, worshiping other gods."

Gomer's mouth fell. Hosea had never used the word *harlot* in her hearing. A feeling of dread rose in her. Tentatively she probed. "Is this not the call you have awaited? Why do you look grieved?"

Hosea lifted his eyes to her. They were filled with such anguish her hand involuntarily flew to her chest, and she knew the use of the word *harlot* had been deliberate. "Has this message from your God anything to do with *me?*" she ventured shakily.

Hosea closed his eyes tightly, as if to shield her from the truth in them. That was answer enough. "Can this be true?" Gomer laid aside the broom. "Do you mean to preach of my past?"

Hosea gently caressed the arms she had bared to gird herself for cleaning. "The Lord God means no harm to you." He swallowed hard. "The Lord means the message to illustrate the sins of His people."

Before he could explain further Gomer pulled away from him and stared in disbelief. "I thought your God was a God of forgiveness," she cried as she flung her arms in hostility. "I thought you said He removes our past. Then why has He chosen to hold me up for ridicule? How can *you* consider doing such a thing to me?"

"I don't understand His purpose either. But I must obey His voice. I ask you to stand with me in this, though I know how you must feel."

"Oh, do you? Then will this empathy keep you from doing this . . . this thing?" Gomer challenged him.

Hosea's arms fell limply at his side.

"Then my reform has been for nothing."

An even deeper grief shaded Hosea's eyes. "Though you have stayed with me these four years, I have watched your heart return to the streets many times. Have you truly reformed?"

Gomer jerked her head back to look at him. He had never accused her before.

"Yes," Hosea said quietly, "I've seen you lured by the call in your heart, beckoning you away. It is no secret from me. And my heart has strained to plea the louder for your allegiance."

"So now you are a seer of the heart?" Gomer snapped, ignoring the truth of his words.

"No, I am not a seer. I only read what was written plainly in your face."

"Then read *this*," Gomer thrust her face up to him, in hopes that her stony countenance would convince him she would not stand for his betrayal.

Hosea cupped her chin in his hands. He traced her features with his finger, and Gomer trembled at his touch. "I read your hurt," he moaned softly. "Oh, God, I wish I were not the cause of your pain!" He closed his eyes and his lips sought out hers.

"No!" Gomer tore herself away. "You have known of this all along, haven't you? That is why you married me! I understand now. You sought to make an example of me. Your God has plotted against me from the beginning. First He took my father, and then the position I worked so hard to gain, and now He would strip away my pride! How can you serve such a one as He?" Gomer's composure crumbled and she sobbed uncontrollably.

Hosea drew close behind her. Laying his hands on her shoulders, he absently massaged them as he cast about in his mind for the right words. "It is true, Gomer, that I knew from the start this day would come. Yet, as each harvest passed, and my love for you grew, I hoped the Lord would turn from His plan. My pain at this is as your own. It is the hardest thing I have ever done."

Gomer clung to her apron, wiping the bitter tears from her face. "How can I believe you anymore?" she choked. "You are no different after all. I almost believed in your God. I almost believed you. It is good that I did not, or I would be utterly destroyed by this. I knew your God was cruel, and now I find you play tricks as wicked as His! I have been a fool to believe in your love." Gomer spat at the storage room wall.

Hosea encircled her with his arms. His eyes blazed more sincerely than they ever had, and he forced her to look into them. "My love for you has always been true. Of *that* there is no question."

"No?" Gomer avoided his gaze. "If you are true to me then refuse to preach this message."

Hosea's face paled and his shoulders drooped. "I cannot refuse God. And you must not, either. If this is His bidding, He will give us strength to endure it together."

"Your God asks too much." Gomer's voice echoed finality.

"No." Hosea's strength of will collided with hers. "He *seems* to ask too much because we never consider giving enough."

Gomer's face hardened. "Hosea, I warn you, if you persist in this betrayal, you will do it at the price of our marriage."

In the passion of torment Hosea grasped the kneading table for stability. *Dear God!* he cried within himself. *I myself cannot believe You would require this of us. Are You immovable?*

The heavens were silent. Hosea breathed deeply,

straining to bring his emotions into subjection. By the time he turned back to his wife he knew, no matter what the price, he would obey the Lord. "Would you ask me to choose between my wife and my God?"

Gomer turned her back on the agony of his suffering, for it threatened to weaken her. How could she consider remaining with him? His mouth spouted words of love even as he betrayed her. Her confidence in Hosea's love was destroyed, and the tender shoot of faith in his God that had begun to sprout withered. *What a fool I was to think this God who ripped my soul apart by taking my father could be loving or have a loving prophet!* Gomer straightened her shoulders. "If asking you to consider me in this matter is causing a choice, then that is what I'm asking."

"I cannot bear this, Gomer. Please don't do this to me!" Hosea pleaded, coming close to embrace her.

Gomer quickly put the kneading table between them. "You?" her voice rose hysterically. "It is *I* who beg *you* not to drive me away!"

Hosea stared at Gomer across the table, heartbroken. She stared back with resolution.

"I see," she said drily. "Do what you must, and I will also."

"It must not be like this." Hosea pounded the table. "I love you, Gomer. *Please* don't leave me!"

Gomer turned her back on him. He knew it was too late. So intense was his grief that it took iron will to set one foot in front of another, to tread the lonely road to the marketplace and deliver his woeful message.

Gomer ran to the door and watched her husband trudge slowly down the street. Arioch appeared on the stairs from the rooftop. The children cowered behind him. Gomer's daughter inched forward. "Where Abba go?" she pleaded with her frightened face lifted to her mother. Gomer stared at her, remembering how she had once asked her mother the same question. *Life is a prison of woe where a hateful God keeps us captive to forever relive our agony,* she decided. Thankfully Arioch interceded, occupying the children with a game of leapfrog, but he kept glancing over his shoulder at Gomer, a worried frown creasing his brow.

Gomer could restrain herself no longer. She ran from the house and followed Hosea. She had to know just how much of her past he would divulge. A huge crowd had already gathered in the marketplace. Gomer stayed at the rear where she could not see her husband but could clearly hear his words.

"And the Lord said to me, 'Go and marry a girl who is a prostitute, so that some of her children will be born to you from other men. This will illustrate the way my people have been untrue to me, committing open adultery against me by worshiping other gods.' "

Gomer grabbed her chest. In their entire marriage Hosea had never once mentioned that Jezreel was not his own. Her head pounded, and her vision blurred with the finality of the scene. She leaned back against a market booth to regain her balance, hearing no more of Hosea's speech. When her vision cleared, hundreds of faces bobbed before her. Her presence had been detected and the crowd was no longer listening to her husband's denouncements. They were gawking at *her.* She was once more a prostitute in their eyes. Like a pack of hungry wolves they licked their lips, delighting in her ruin.

Despair engulfed her. She desperately clutched at the booth and her hand lighted on a wooden carving of Baal.

Her fist tightened around it. An idea formed in her mind, sending flames shooting from her eyes that could have reduced the wooden trinket to ashes.

Gomer looked back at the crowd and found the people had cleared an aisle between her and her husband. She almost broke under his loving gaze, but vengeance consumed her, and she slowly lifted the carving to him. She enbraced the idol with a kiss, then stalked away.

18

Their mother has committed adultery. She did a shameful thing when she said, "I'll run after other men and sell myself to them for food and drinks and clothes." . . . She put on her earrings and jewels and went out looking for her lovers, and deserted me.

Hosea 2:5,13

Gomer did not know how she reached the chambers where she and Hosea slept. Leaning heavily against the threshold to catch her breath, her memory buzzed with a muddled recollection of kicking at clamoring dogs that yapped at her feet as she mounted the stairs to the roof. With a stab of guilt she realized the dogs had been her children.

Her guilt was quickly swallowed by the numbing pain of humiliation. *I have watched your heart return to the streets many times, many times. . . .* Hosea's accusation haunted her. She shook her head and her gaze settled on her bed mat, rolled neatly in the corner with a scented linen sheet folded on top of it. She scooped up the sheet, the only luxury belonging to her, renting it apart as God had rent apart her marriage. Sweat poured down her face. She gulped bittersweet sobs, tasting the rose scent of the linen mixed with her briny tears.

Her attention focused on the myrtle twig she had saved from her wedding night. She gripped only a bare stalk, for the flowers had faded and crumbled long ago. *Withered like our love. I should have taken a lesson from the myrtle branch.* Gomer began furiously beating Hosea's sleeping mat. *How I hate you!* She slashed it savagely.

Her mind reeled like the disc of a grinding wheel while Hosea's taunting words ricocheted in the confusion of her soul. *I have watched your heart return to the streets, to the streets . . . Of course.* The old determination returned to her face as she began rummaging for her long-ignored cosmetics and jewelry. *The prophet has prophesied his wife's future.*

As her mind cleared to focus on applying her thick makeup she could hear the children crying downstairs. Guilt pricked her again, but she pursed her lips in an effort to close her heart. The room became suffocating. The air was heavy with humidity, and the walls seemed about to topple and crush her. Gomer's eyes swept the cubicle. *In this room he almost made me believe him. But his love was a lie.* Pain stabbed her heart again, and she ran from the room.

Arioch met her at the foot of the stairs with the children. "Pretty Mamma!" Lo-ruhamah dried her tears, pointing at Gomer's made-up face. Suddenly Gomer's jewelry weighed so heavy that it threatened to pull her to her knees. Lo-ruhamah's shining face threatened to trap her here. Her son's eyes beseeched her. Gomer sought for a defense against them.

"Gomer, surely you are not—" Arioch stopped because of the children's presence.

"Why not? Isn't that what Hosea has foretold for me?"

Her eyes flashed from rage to purpose as the defense she sought formed. She moved like a cat slinking toward its prey. With slow, panting breaths she pressed her body into him and dug her lioness claws into the flesh of Arioch's shoulders. Her mouth twisted grotesquely as she forced it against his.

Grabbing Gomer's wrists, Arioch pulled them from around his neck. He pushed her away and slapped her. The force of the slap directed her gaze into the confused faces of her children. By the hurt in their eyes she knew she had cut them off from her. *There, it's done. They couldn't love me now, and I'm glad. If they don't love me I don't have to worry about loving them. They are better off without me anyway.*

Finally touching her throbbing cheek she looked at Arioch. "Tell Hosea his prophecy was wrong. It's not to the streets I return." Gomer bit her lip and brushed past Arioch, leaving her home without a backward glance.

19

Yes, I have seen a horrible thing in Israel—Ephraim chasing other gods, Israel utterly defiled. . . . Their love for shame is greater than for honor. . . . Your deeds won't let you come to God again, for the spirit of adultery is deep within you, and you cannot know the Lord.

Hosea 6:10; 4:18; 5:4

"Halt!" barked the guard at the palace gate. "What is your purpose here?"

"That is an apt question," Gomer answered gruffly, matching his authoritative tone. "But I believe if you announce my presence to the king, he will allow me entrance." She drew her form up to full height, showing the guard something of her own command. He did not seem impressed. *Here I am, once more fighting a power struggle,* Gomer thought wearily. *I wonder if it will be the same with Menahem.*

The guard eyed her suspiciously before he commanded a servant to send word to the king. Gomer rested against the gatepost, emptied of the anger and humiliation that had propelled her from her home. Blindly wandering the city until sunset had served to cool her hostile wrath to the point of simmering revenge. *I will show Hosea and his God I don't need them. I can make a way for myself. Menahem wanted me once; I will make sure he does again.*

The servant returned and whispered something to the guard. Without a word he opened the gate to let Gomer in. The servant led her to the banquet hall where, over six years ago, she had been presented to Jeroboam. A huge statue of Baal now monopolized the center of the room. Its eyes were of onyx and a golden lightning bolt was gripped in its upraised arm. Though the hall was overflowing with boisterous guests and music resounded in the court, a reverence for the idol muted the sounds.

Tonight is the yearly feast, Gomer remembered, imagining Hosea residing over the table in the little house snuggled close to the walls of Samaria. She envisioned Jezreel proudly reciting the lines she had helped him memorize and instantly refused the thought that she missed them. *I will show Hosea,* she reminded herself.

Gomer became aware that Menahem was watching her. She turned and moved slowly toward him. He was presiding regally on the ivory throne of Jeroboam, his muscular frame decorated with vesture of golden lacework and silks of purple and gold. His bare arm flashed a royal band of bronze and topaz. He wore kingship more awesomely than when she had seen him last. The familiar excitement of his presence rose within her breast, but doubts assailed her. *Will he still desire me? Will he reject me, thinking my presence here signals his victory in our personal battle? I must be clever if I am to win his affections.*

"What is it you want?" Menahem motioned Gomer closer to him. His face did not even reveal recognition.

"I came for the celebration." Gomer's lips were tight as she spoke. She wiped the sweat from her forehead.

Hosea wiped a tear from his eye. He lowered a dripping hyssop branch and inspected the lintel and two side panels of his doorway. Bright red blood hid the darkened stains of past feasts celebrated in the house and contrasted sharply with the unstained doorposts of neighboring homes.

His lips moved silently as he consecrated the house, and another tear trickled down his cheek. It had been only an hour since he returned from preaching in the marketplace to be told Gomer had fled. He could not believe she was gone. He had to believe she would return.

Revealing her fear had been a mistake. Menahem laughed at her. "For the celebration?" he repeated. "Have you been invited?" Giggles were heard around the room. Menahem was enjoying this.

Gomer stared at him sullenly. "Yes, I have been invited by the king, but the invitation is old and has lain forgotten in my heart for many years."

"Indeed." Menahem nodded his head approvingly at her answer. To his servant he instructed, "Make a place for her, there." He pointed to the place of lowest honor in the banquet hall, challenging Gomer with his eyes.

Gomer bristled at the insult, but murmured, "My thanks for your kindness."

As Gomer took her seat more servants extinguished the lamps one by one, exchanging their light for the eerie glow of candles. Gomer's presence was forgotten. The rhythmic whine of a lone lyre drifted into the room accompanying the wriggling form of a young girl dropping veils as she danced. She whirled around the statue of

Baal three times as the lyre was joined by a harp, tambourine, and other instruments.

Gomer had searched for a way to win Menahem over, and recognizing the sacrificial movements of the dance, she knew her moment had come. Snatching up the scattered veils of the dancer she gave the girl a shove, usurping her place in the ritual.

The small family was seated around a low wooden table with one empty cushion. The house was dark, lit only by candles. Four-year-old Jezreel stood and approached his father. Hosea put his arm around him and began.

"The Lord said to Moses and Aaron, 'From now on, this month will be the first and most important month of the Jewish calendar. Annually, on the tenth day of this month each family shall get a lamb. This animal shall be a year-old male, either a sheep or a goat, without any defects. On the evening of the fourteenth day of this month, all these lambs shall be killed, and their blood shall be placed on the two side-frames of the door of every home and on the panel above the door. Use the blood of the lamb eaten in that home. Everyone shall eat roast lamb that night, with unleavened bread and bitter herbs. Don't eat any of it the next day; if all is not eaten that night, burn what is left.

" 'Eat it with your traveling clothes on, prepared for a long journey, wearing your walking shoes and carrying your walking sticks in your hands; eat it hurriedly. This observance shall be called the Lord's Passover. You shall celebrate this event each year (this is a permanent law) to remind you of this fatal night.' "

Jezreel cleared his throat and his childish voice piped the lines he had rehearsed all week with his mother.

"What does all this mean, Father? What is this ceremony about?"

"It is the celebration of God's passing over us, for He passed over the homes of the people of Israel, though He killed the Egyptians." Hosea delivered the words of the ceremony, but his prayers were with Gomer. *Please pass over Gomer this night, El Shaddai, and grant her mercy. Bring her home.* Even as he spoke the sacred words over the meal, his heart longed for Gomer's return to spare him this agony. Hosea was glad the darkness hid his tears.

The dancing girl was furious at Gomer's interruption. She grabbed Gomer's hair and spit on her. Menahem ordered her removed with the flick of a wrist and watched with interest as Gomer courted the room with her dance. His eyes shone greedily as she moved sensuously toward him.

Gomer knew well the meaning of her movements. The ritual dance meant she was offering her body to the king in payment for the continued blessing of Baal on the fertility of the land. She pulled the veils provocatively over her body. Drawing closer to the throne, she made lewd, enticing gestures. Suddenly Menahem stood. Lifting his wine chalice he gave the signal that Baal had accepted the sacrifice and for Gomer to be sent to his chambers to complete the fertility rite.

Gomer was ecstatic. *Soon I will be the most exalted woman in Israel. How could I have ever considered the confining existence Hosea offered? This is what I have been longing for. This is the life I was destined for.*

As the family ate the meat and herbs silently and hurriedly, Hosea tasted their bitterness more than ever, for now bitterness came also from his heart.

How could she do this to me? he thought and slammed down his wine cup, startling his family. Lois and Arioch exchanged glances, then looked at him sympathetically. Hosea was oblivious. *I have given of myself all these years and yet that was not enough to prove my love to her. What more could I have done?* He choked on his lamb at the thought that her feelings for him were so shallow she would desert him. No matter how it hurt her, after all his years of sacrifice for her, she could endure this one trial for him.

She will surely feel God's wrath for her unfaithfulness! Hosea was almost glad at the thought. But he soothed his conscience with a forced prayer for her. He leaned back from the table, justifying his bitterness with righteous retribution.

With hunger in his eyes Menahem led Gomer to his canopied bed. As they lay together, completing the sacrifice, he was almost violent. If Gomer had not voluntarily submitted to him, she would have felt raped. In the midst of Menahem's warlike advances Gomer could not keep the memory of Hosea's tenderness from her thoughts. But she set her jaw and told herself it was worth the king's abuses to gain the life only he could offer her.

When Menahem was done with her he lay back and stared at the canopy, satisfied. "Ah, but the spoils of war are sweet," he breathed. There was an air of victory about him that infuriated Gomer.

"I am not booty! And you have not won me. I came of my own will. If there were a war between us, what makes you so confident you would be the victor? In love, rank is not the superior weapon."

Suddenly Menahem was on top of her, clenching both her wrists. "If I had not taken you now, I would have taken you later," he growled. "*I* decide what I want and when I will take it. And I *always* win. Do you understand, woman?"

Gomer's face distorted with sarcasm. "Oh, can you ever forgive me, my lord. I spoke with haste. And do you want this lowly servant to wash your feet for you also?"

Menahem stared at her. His eyes lost their mirage-like appeal. They were stone cold. "Yes, I do." A wicked smile parted his lips. He threw her to the floor and thrust his feet in her face.

20

Court her again. . . . O Jezreel, rename your brother and sister. . . . for now God will have mercy.

Hosea 2:14,1

Hosea sat brooding on the west ridge of the verdant Mount Carmel. His eyes swept the pastel plains below, dotted with trees that looked like puffs of green wool backed by the blue mist of the Great Sea. The sun blazed orange above it, giving the landscape the effect of an inverted rainbow.

He had hoped that camping on this holy place where Elijah challenged the prophets of Baal over a century ago would somehow encourage him. *Elijah managed to sway the people with a prayer and a miracle; why can't I?* Hosea pouted. He kicked a stone and watched it roll down the mountain.

For five years he had preached El Shaddai's message, and in his heart he felt the years were wasted. Though he desired to serve his God he knew he was insufficient for the task. Even the words of Amos prophesying his lack and God's abundance no longer soothed him. *I am but twenty-nine winters and already a failure.* Hosea kicked at another loose stone.

Not only did his preaching lack results, but the fact that his service to God accomplished nothing but to keep him from his family added to his torment. Always he calculated the distance to Samaria. Mount Carmel was three days' journey from his home. *Home.* He pondered the treasure of its memory, kept hidden in his bosom, and the questions seared him again. How could home be the same without his wife to share it? *Gomer, why did you leave? How could my love and El Shaddai not be enough for you? How could you leave me and reject all I offered?* Still he prayed for her, fasted for her, and most of all, loved her. *But what is the use? Have I not failed there also?*

Hosea remembered how the rejected Elijah wished death after Jezebel threatened his life, and how he fled into the wilderness to pray for God to take him. "I too have felt rejection, El Shaddai," Hosea spoke aloud. "There is nothing more I can do. I have obeyed Your word and nothing has come of it. I do not question You, for I am the one who has failed. Take me and spare Israel the trouble."

Hosea's shoulders slumped in defeat. He stood and decided to go back to the cave where he was camped. There he would wait to die as the prophet of old. He followed an ancient path and came to the place where Elijah once repaired the altar of the Lord. Indignation filled Hosea at the sight of its dismantled condition. *The people have destroyed Your altar again. How can You bear it, El Shaddai?* As he thought of the pain God must endure from the people's rejection of Him, Hosea yearned to renew his own dedication and soothe God by proclaiming his love before he died.

He gathered twelve large stones to represent the twelve

tribes of Israel and repaired the altar, just as Elijah had done. After gathering twigs and brush he placed them on top of the altar, then snared a wild goat for a sacrifice.

As the smell of singed flesh filled his nostrils, his heart burned to renew his confession of love for God. *"Shema Yisroel Adonoy Elohenu, Adonoy Echod!* Hear O Israel, the Lord our God, the Lord is One!" Hosea stretched out his arms toward the sky and tears streamed down his cheeks. He knew God's wayward people would not hear. "Elijah made it so simple when he said, 'If the Lord is God, follow him. But if Baal is God, then follow him.' If no one else will, *I* will follow You, my Lord!"

When nothing was left of the sacrifice but ashes, Hosea left silently for the cave. He halted when he heard the sound of a gentle whisper. "Court her again—"

"But I did, and she rejected me," Hosea objected. Hosea could not believe what he heard and covered his ears, but the voice would not be cut off.

"Court her again, and bring her into the wilderness—"

"But, El Shaddai," Hosea whined, "she rejected *You* too."

The voice continued. "And speak to her tenderly there."

"El Shaddai!" Hosea's voice was full of despair. "I love Gomer, but she took my love and ground it beneath her feet. She spit on me and offered herself to another man. Shouldn't she be the one to come back to me?"

Hosea was grieved to hear his own words of unforgiveness. He had never admitted to bitterness, but now God was bringing it to light. He could not deny his sin. God's voice was silent, waiting. Then the breath of His Spirit moved the winds across the mountainside. *Do you love Gomer? Or have you measured love in portion as a man does, according to the amount returned?*

Hosea was overwhelmed with shame. "It is true; I

have deceived myself," he wept. "I have withheld love, fearing another failure."

If I have sent you, why do you take the weight of failure on yourself, unless it is to also take the credit of success when it comes?

"I am a wicked man." Hosea threw a handful of dirt into the air above his head. "I have not truly loved Gomer or my country. I fear you have chosen the wrong one to show Israel Your love." Yet even as he spoke he knew he was God's choice. "I don't know *how* to love them," he cried.

"Court her again." The winds of the Lord scattered a solace of love into every hidden crevice of the mountain, bending trees as it passed and bending Hosea's will as it swept over him. "And bring her into the wilderness, and speak to her tenderly there."

Hosea was still perplexed. "If my love was wrong, then how *do* I love her?"

The Spirit of God answered. *Your love was not wrong; it was not enough.*

Hosea's countenance lit with a smile. "But God is called El Shaddai. *He* is enough!" A cloud lifted in his soul and he glimpsed into the ways of God's love. The Lord had told him to rename Lo-ammi and call him Ammi, which means, *Now you are Mine,* and to call Lo-ruhamah, Ruhamah, which means, *Pitied,* for God would have mercy. On his knees he marveled at the love and patience of El Shaddai. He worshiped his Lord for the truth he had been shown.

Like the illumination of lightning Hosea recalled his hesitancy to tell Gomer he must use their marriage as an illustration of Israel's unfaithfulness. *God's love is not afraid of truth. Even if truth wounds in the beginning, it heals in the end. If I had not tried to shield Gomer from hurt with apologies and doubts, she might have found repentance. She would have seen the choice before her, as clearly as Elijah set the same choice before the people. With my human concept of love, I put myself in the path of God.*

"I am at fault for doubting You." Hosea covered his face with his hands and whispered, "Forgive me."

21

*P*lead *with your mother, for she has become another
man's wife—I am no longer her husband. Beg her to stop her
harlotry, to quit giving herself to others. . . . But I will court
her again, and bring her into the wilderness, and speak to her
tenderly there. . . . She will respond to me there.*

Hosea 2:2,14,15

Stationed on her veranda, Gomer peered through the
trees of her olive grove and into the hazy valley below
Samaria. *How beautiful you look, and how deceptive
you are*, she mentally addressed the terrain. She felt akin
to the distant perfection that hid the barrenness of the
valley. *I know what it is like to hide beneath beauty.*

Set high in the royal quarters, surrounded by gifts of
luxury and living from feast to feast, Gomer longed for
more. *I have it all, yet I still want, and I cannot even
name what I seek. What more is there?* Gomer again consulted the god of clay she held in the palm of her hand.
Insulted by its silence, she slung it from the veranda. Earrings and amulets made a sparkling arch in the sun as she
stripped herself of them and tossed them down also. *Of
what value are jewels if they no longer give pleasure?* She
consoled herself with the knowledge that she had plenty

more jewels to throw away if she so chose. *There is no lasting pleasure in riches,* Gomer thought as she kicked off her anklet and watched its descent down the hillside.

It would take more than discarding a few trinkets to cast off the deceptive layer of luxury she hid beneath. Even without the accessories she knew her dress and manner would mark her as one of the royal court. Her long hair was braided into an Egyptian coiffure, and her flowing gown of fine, white linen was draped with embroidered silks and belted with golden threads. She carried herself like a proud, stately column, unaffected by sorrow, but she was a lie.

Gomer heard familiar footsteps behind her. Ka'Tan bowed at the entrance to her room. His age was beginning to tell, but his regal appearance endured. Even the gray that speckled his hair seemed to add sophistication. *My faithful servant seems to live only to serve me. Sometimes I think he is the greatest of all the gifts from the king. Ah, the king . . .* Gomer could not seem to quiet her thoughts. *Entertaining Menahem for the past five years has earned all my wealth, but if I become boring in his eyes I could lose it all. Is it worth it?* She was beginning to wonder.

Ka'Tan stood silently awaiting permission to speak, but his lips rounded in a secretive gesture. "A young man asks to be presented," he said with a smile when Gomer gestured him forward. Ka'Tan nodded to someone behind her door. A nine-year-old boy hesitantly entered.

"Jezreel?" Gomer speculated momentarily on her son's presence. The past seemed to eat away at the present, and a forgotten fear replaced the vague longings she had been experiencing. "What brings you here?" she said too sharply, in an attempt to mask the feelings her son stirred in her.

"Father sent me," Jezreel stated flatly.

"Of course." There seemed to be nothing else to say.

"Father instructed me to give you this." The boy handed Gomer a shard. She made a face at the indecipherable scratches on the piece of broken pottery and passed it to Ka'Tan.

"Read it," she demanded, "aloud."

Ka'Tan began. " 'My beloved Gomer. Rise, my love, and come away with me while the renewal of spring beckons with its approach.' " Ka'Tan paused, embarrassed, but Gomer urged him on. " 'The lilies of the field glaze the winter grass and birds sing in the skies overhead. Come, let us renew our love along with all creation.' "

Gomer leaned forward. "Is that all?" Ka'Tan nodded. She placed her hands on her hips and laughed. "Does he yet believe I will return to him? Where is he? Jezreel, send for him."

Jezreel scurried out, returning with his father. Hosea obviously had been awaiting the invitation. Gomer held her breath at the sight of him. Five years of traversing the country had bronzed his skin and had added an alluring ruggedness to his features. His eyes held an attractive assurance.

"Well?"

"What?" Gomer had been so distracted by Hosea's presence she forgot why he was there.

"My message." He nodded toward the shard in Ka'-Tan's hand.

"Oh, yes." Gomer took on a business-like manner to camouflage her pounding heart. "May we talk a little before I send you away?"

"You won't send me away."

Hosea's bold advances unnerved her. Her voice trembling, she inquired, "How are the children?" Gomer envisioned three children clinging to Hosea, pleading for her return.

"I've renamed them." Even as Hosea spoke of their children his eyes spoke of their reunion.

Gomer changed the subject. "Is this some new trick of your God, sending children as forerunners before his prophets? Was the sight of my child supposed to weaken me? On the contrary, Hosea, his presence reminded me of how you have told the world he is not your child."

"Sending Jezreel was my idea." Hosea lifted mischievous eyes to her. "But it seems to have succeeded."

Gomer crossed her arms. "Simply because I allowed you entrance to my home, it does not follow that I will allow more. Just look about you, Hosea. I don't need you anymore. I have my own household gods, my own vineyards, my own oil and grain—I even own this house filled with servants. The king has showered me with treasures and my position as his consort serves me well. Would you seek to call me away from such happiness?"

"Are you happy, Gomer?" Hosea asked, doubtful.

"Of course." She laughed and inwardly marveled at how well she had learned to pretend. "Remember how you once saved me from Menahem? It seems he is now the redeemer. How I longed for salvation from the boredom of your arms, and Menahem set me free." Gomer watched Hosea closely for signs of pain. She wanted to hurt him as much as he had her. "Shall I tell you how I respond to *Menahem's* embrace? Shall I repeat for you the words of love *he* whispers in my ear?"

Hosea looked sternly at Gomer then patted Jezreel's shoulder. "Son, go home now." The boy left silently, followed discreetly by Ka'Tan.

"Jealousy becomes you, Hosea," Gomer said haughtily.

"My jealousy is not because of Menahem, for I know the evil purposes of the king have been thwarted by El Shaddai to serve His own. If Menahem conquers, El Shaddai first wills it."

"Are you so deceived?" Gomer was incredulous. "The king did not take me for evil, but for pleasure. And I have given him much of it, Hosea."

Hosea said nothing.

"Another man takes your wife and you cannot show jealousy? I seem to recall a great many speeches from you, pledging me your never-ending love. I knew they were all lies." Gomer's lips curved contemptuously.

"Jealousy is not foreign to me, Gomer. I would discuss that and many other things with you, but not here." He touched her arm and Gomer could not pull away. "Listen to your heart for a moment and come with me. I know you want to."

Gomer could not resist the promise of tenderness she had longed for these many years away from her husband.

"Are you afraid to speak, my love?" Hosea stroked her cheek. "Are you fearful that your words might reflect what has remained silent within your heart? Then do not speak, only give me your hand."

"You wanted to know if I am jealous?" Hosea resumed their conversation as he reclined against a willow, absently rolling a twig between his hands. Rays of sunlight filtered through the crowns of majestic trees lending enchantment to the hillside of Samaria. The forest foliage seemed to encircle them as securely as a womb. A dove cooed in the branches overhead. "I am jealous only for you." He waited for a reply, but there was none.

Hosea watched as Gomer unbraided her hair and let

the long curls tumble over her tawny shoulders. He looked into Gomer's black eyes. They seemed to have grown beyond maturity into agelessness, holding all the secrets of a primeval forest. "Gomer, how I longed for your touch these past years, and now you sit before me like clusters of grapes in the wilderness, tempting me to harvest your delights." Gomer lifted her hair back and tilted her face to the sky, but said nothing. Hosea threw down the twig he was holding. "Will you never change?" he asked disgustedly.

Gomer breathed deeply of the forest air and thought she detected the scent of rain. She sighed. "Why do you not like me as I am? I have often wondered what our marriage would have been like if you hadn't been constantly expecting me to change."

"But I never asked that of you," Hosea blurted. "I only asked that you listen to your heart. I never required your repentance, I only hoped for it."

Gomer turned her head to hide her shimmering eyes. "But I did listen to my heart, and that has caused only confusion. You fulfilled in me the kind of love I only dreamed about before, but, somehow," she turned back to Hosea, "it was not enough. Menahem promised love of a different kind, exciting and prosperous, but it has not been enough either. How can I listen to my heart when I no longer trust it?"

Hosea took her hand. "You will continue to be torn between us until you choose between us. That is what I came to tell you, and what I should have told you from the start. The choice is clear, but, like Israel, you resist the love of God, thinking you will find something better elsewhere. In the end you forfeit the best: El Shaddai."

Gomer sighed again. "You always talk about *Him*. Perhaps *I* should be the one who is jealous." She looked beyond the tops of the trees to a place Hosea could not see. "Your God called to me once, when Abba died. But I sent Him away." For a moment she looked almost sorry.

"You may have sent Him away, but He will never leave you. It is not too late." Hosea shook with expectancy. "We could still love Him together."

"Look how you tremble at His name." Gomer's eyes swept his frame. "No doubt I *should* be jealous."

Hosea was exasperated with Gomer's evasions. He lay in a pile of old leaves and placed his hands under his head. He watched the sunlight play in the treetops and said, "Gomer, you must make a choice. Let me help you. Tell me how I can make you forget your other lover. Tell me what I can do to bind you to me, to make you choose *me*." His voice softened and he looked intently at her. "Oh, Gomer, let us forget there has ever been another and let this be the dawn of our love. As El Shaddai lives, I swear my heart belongs to you. If you decide against us, the memory of you will remain as a monument to a possibility. What could have been with you at my side will torture me forever.

"Listen to me, I beg you! Forget the past. I already have. I know you think I am a fool, but it does not matter. I am drunk with love, but I do not wish to clear my head. Gomer, do you not see? I am yours, and I want you to be mine."

She smiled at him. "You make it hard to refuse."

"Then don't." Hosea's hopes soared.

"Hosea," Gomer leaned over him, her loosened curls caressing his face. "Is it true? Can you really love me like this, even after . . ."

"Yes, I do love you. God's love is never-ending."

"But is love the only thing of importance?" Gomer nearly whispered as she wrestled with her desires. "Is it enough to—"

190

"God is enough!" Hosea laughed. "He loves you so, Gomer, and I do too. You are the only woman I have ever loved." He smiled and gently twirled a curl around his finger. "You and a dream."

"A dream?"

"Yes, but the dream was a lie I chased for nothing. I only discovered a nightmare at the end of it."

"I chase a dream also. But I have not yet found its fulfillment."

"I did not find the end of my dream through searching. God revealed it to me. What is it you seek, Gomer?" Hosea sat up and looked at her.

She looked at him sadly. "You offer your love so freely to me and I have rejected it, but it *is* love I seek."

Hosea's head drooped. "Have I failed you that much?" He looked up and sought comfort in her face. There was none. He reached for her hand. "What more can I do, Gomer? Tell me and I will—" Suddenly his eyes brightened. "Wait here."

"Hosea!" Gomer called in alarm as he dashed without warning into the forest thicket. "Don't leave me here alone." She glanced about, and the serene forest suddenly seemed oppressive. She sat very still for what seemed an eternity and thought she heard a wildcat's gutteral call not too far distant. Thunder rumbled overhead and a raindrop fell on her nose.

"Hosea!" she screeched, but there was no answer. She panicked. *This is a trap. He left me here to die.* A small fox skirted past her, and Gomer screamed in hysteria.

"Gomer." Hosea's voice came from behind her.

She ran to him crying and embraced him tightly. "Don't ever leave me like that again."

As Gomer continued to cling to him, sobbing like a frightened child, Hosea realized how lost she was, and how desperately she needed to be found. He soothed her.

"Oh, my love, you need me much more than you know."

Finally she loosened her grip enough to peer up at him, brushing away tears with the back of her hand. "Why did you leave me?"

"Believe me, if I had known how it would frighten you, I would not have left." Hosea held up a wreath of white anemones and placed it lovingly on her head. He flashed a boyish grin. "I made it for you. It is a symbol for a new beginning. Our beginning."

"How do you know I will choose you when I'm not sure myself?"

"I don't." Hosea adjusted the wreath and kissed her forehead. "But an hour ago you were ready to send me away. And now . . ." He held out his hand to her and she grasped it. He led her down a faint path through the woods to a clearing.

The clouds momentarily parted to allow the sun to trickle through the dense foliage and touch them with its warmth. A seasonal brook lined with the same anemones Hosea had used for the wreath bubbled its way through the center of the glen. Fragrant aloes and terebinth trees framed the moss-carpeted vale. At the edge of the clearing, an elusive rock partridge gave its familiar call, then darted into a dense tamarisk bush. A few raindrops splattered, making the shelter offered by the tall trees of the grove inviting.

"This is a lover's garden." Hosea smiled and his intent was reflected in the twinkle of his eyes. "El Shaddai has tended it just for us. Here we may take the fill of our love, Gomer."

Gomer leaned against a fig tree beside the stream and felt the cool refreshment of the delicate shower. She closed her eyes. "This is how I always imagined Egypt would be. How I would love to see it with my own eyes."

Hosea shook his head and slung a rock into the brook, disrupting the ceremonial silence of the clearing with its force. The shower increased in measure. He raised his voice to match the hiss of steadily falling rain. "Must you be a silly dove always flying somewhere new? Should I cast a net over you like I would a bird in the sky and bring you down from your flight of fantasy?" Rain poured over his face from his drenched hair as he appealed to her with his arms outstretched. "Touch me, Gomer. I'm not a woven dream of yours, I am flesh and blood. I offer you my love. Leave me again for Menahem if you must, but don't cast me aside for a dream!"

She narrowed her eyes. Anger forced her to face him through the driving rain. The elegant chiton clung to Gomer and her hair dripped in her eyes. "Once I asked you not to choose your God over me. You refused. Now you ask me to choose between you and Menahem, between my gods and your God, between dreams and reality. I have heard enough of—" Gomer stomped and lost her footing on the mossy bank of the stream. Quickly Hosea reached to steady her, but his foot caught on an outgrown tree root and he succeeded only in making her lose her balance completely. Clutching awkwardly at Hosea, Gomer pulled him down with her. They slid precariously down the sloped bank into the brook, landing with a splash. Hosea was the first to break the astonished silence. His animated laughter drowned out even the driving rain. Gomer tried very hard not to, but soon her throaty merriment filled the forest with its sound.

Hosea pushed Gomer's saturated hair back from her face and straightened the mangled wreath. His brow creased with fervency. "I *so* desire your love, Gomer. I always will." He pulled her close. "It's stopped raining," he noted and Gomer inspected the sky for proof. A rainbow arched its way over the clearing and canopied them with color and promise.

Gomer drew circles in the beads of water glistening on Hosea's forehead. "The choice would be easy if I could hate you."

Hosea smiled and carried her out of the stream. He sat her carefully beside the water and gently unlatched her sandals, then pillowed her head with the mossy bank, allowing the water of the brook to blanket her feet. Leaning over her he tenderly kissed her.

Even as their love seemed to take root, entwining itself in the purity and privacy of the tranquil, flowing stream, Hosea wondered if she would leave him again. Though Gomer fully responded to him he knew the reawakening of their love risked new wounds for them both. But he had known the pain of apathy and how it could embitter one's heart. He had made *his* choice.

22

The very arrogance of Israel testifies against her in my court. She will stumble under her load of guilt.

Hosea 5:5

Why can't Hosea be more like Menahem? Gomer sighed. She stared wistfully out the window beside her old perch on the stairs leading to their room on the roof. *Or would I rather Menahem be more like Hosea? I don't know anymore. This man has me so confused. To what does he bid me with his kisses? To sit upon stairs while life races past me?* Gomer heaved another dissatisfied sigh. Three days of boredom in Hosea's humble dwelling had magnified her longings. *Hosea's lips drip with a sweet passion I have always dreamed of, but his desirability ceases there. I cannot live on his love alone. If I am going to leave, I must do it soon. The longer I stay the more I will hurt him and the children too.* Gomer winced at the thought of her children. They treated her as they would a guest. *But is that not my desire?* she reminded herself.

"Lois! Lois!" Arioch shouted breathlessly, throwing open the door. Gomer had been religiously ignored by

Hosea's family, especially Arioch, since she came back, and she returned the scorn. She presumed herself as far above them as her perch on the stairs. Studiously she faced the window, belying her interest in the usually reserved man's outburst.

"What is it?" Lois hovered about her brother anxiously.

Arioch gasped, "Hosea. They took him."

Gomer shot down the steps and grabbed Arioch's arm. "Who took him?"

"Soldiers, from the palace. They took him to prison!" Hosea's brother was quivering with trepidation. Lois covered her mouth with both her hands, her eyes bulging hysterically above them.

"Did they say why?" Gomer seemed the only one in control amid the panic.

"No," Arioch said, waving his arms for emphasis. "They just said he was under arrest."

Before he could finish, Gomer swung out the door, a determined gait speeding her steps to the palace. She could hear Lois clicking her tongue. "I am glad the children are playing so they do not see their mother desert them again. She won't be back, you know."

"Out of my way!" Gomer demanded. "The king is expecting me."

Gomer stopped at the entrance to the throne room. No woman was allowed to enter unless beckoned by the king. Her mouth tightened at the sight of Menahem. "What have you done with him?"

Menahem examined the ivory head of his scepter, brushing imaginary dust from its crevices. "Has this woman been sent for?" he inquired of a nearby attendant.

Gomer strode across the room and up to the foot of the throne, defying the law that forbade her entrance. "Yes, I have been sent for. In your typical childish way you have summoned me here."

"I should have you slain, woman!" Menahem growled. "Do you not have the wits to know it is the king you speak to?"

"It is not the king I address, but a jealous little boy who is playing tricks to gain my attention."

"You will speak to me with a respectful tongue, whore!" Menahem bolted from his podium.

Gomer shouted with equal threat. "I command you to release my husband."

"You command *me* to—?" Menahem sputtered and his hooked nose flared till the veins in it were revealed. His face was the color of a smelting oven, and Gomer brought her face close to it.

"There is nothing more you can do to hurt me. Your threats are useless now, lord of Israel. By your own tactics you have lost this war."

Menahem raised his scepter to strike her. Gomer stood taller. "Yes, kill me," her eyes sparked insolently. "Or let me live and imprison me also. It doesn't matter. Either way you have lost."

The king's arm froze in midair. Suddenly he laughed and threw his scepter across the room. "Excellent. You are a cunning witch, Gomer. But that is how I like you." He walked slowly around her, pulling on his lower lip. "And you are right about the way I summoned for you, but you are wrong about the war. I am not fighting you. Rather I sport with you. You are a clever opponent, and I derive as much pleasure from the game as from knowing I will win."

Gomer stood rigid as Menahem strutted around her.

"Who else can win when you conceive the rules as it pleases you?"

Menahem pressed his forefingers to his mouth and nodded. "There is some truth to that. But have you not made a few new rules yourself?"

"I want my husband released."

Menahem turned to his court and spread his arms palms upward, the sleeve of his robe touching the floor. "Is she not delightful?" There were knowing nods and snickers in return.

"I did not come here for your pleasure," Gomer stomped and shouted angrily.

"Now, now," Menahem shook his finger at her. "You must not lose control of your temper. It reduces you to the rank of a peasant and puts you at a disadvantage." Menahem paused and looked thoughtfully at the carved ceiling. He assumed a taunting sneer. "I like that. Don't lose control," he quoted himself. "I think I'll make that a new rule."

When his goading produced no reaction in Gomer he went on. "You know, you muddle your concentration by playing at two games at once."

Gomer wanted only to discuss Hosea's release, but she was familiar with the king's tactics. If she did not play along he would quickly tire of her and both she and Hosea would be forgotten in the palace dungeon. *Why am I risking my life for a man I am considering leaving forever?* The thought flashed through her mind but she dismissed it. *Hosea must not suffer innocently for my involvement with Menahem.*

"Suppose," she tilted her head coyly, "it is you who are at a disadvantage. You play at a different game than I. You play a game of chase. But can one be chased who does not run? Who then is muddled?"

"Very good," Menahem lowered his head respectfully

198

toward Gomer. "But it seems I gave you credit for more intelligence than I should. I do not chase, but hunt as the fowler." He intertwined his fingers in Gomer's hair. "And you, my dear witless little dove, have flown straight into my snare." His fist tightened painfully on her thick tresses and his arm trembled in the effort to bring her to her knees. "That's right, my little jackal, resist until the end." Gomer locked her knees in a valiant effort to remain standing, but Menahem's strength overcame her.

He loomed overhead, his feet spread in a victorious stance, staring down at her. "You dared to walk out on the king. To reject me for a skinny, whining prophet. I, the king," Menahem thumped his chest and glared around the court full of his subjects, "will allow such arrogance from no one. Least of all a woman!"

"Ask my forgiveness," he demanded.

Gomer spat on his arm.

"WOMAN!" he roared the word like a wounded, wild animal. The entire court trembled. Menahem looked down at Gomer, still in his grip. His eyes danced with a sinister flame. Without looking from her he commanded a nearby servant. "Bring me Hosea's head."

"No!" Gomer screamed.

Menahem smiled. He released his grip on her but she remained kneeling. "I said you had flown into my trap. You did not believe me, eh?" He paced before her, looking at her sideways. He stopped and spread his feet again in a commanding motion. "You want Hosea spared? Ask my forgiveness."

Gomer's body trembled. She looked down. "Will you—"

"Louder!" the king shouted. "And look at me when you speak."

Tears coursed down Gomer's face. "Will the lord of

Israel pardon his servant?" she slowly slung at him, enunciating every word clearly as her eyes filled with blood-chilling hate. She killed the lingering hope of finding her childhood dream-lover in him.

"Is that all?" Menahem crossed his arms.

Gomer knew what he wanted her to say, and she knew she could not. *But I cannot let Hosea die.* She swallowed hard. "My lord, you are without equal. I was an idiot to have fled from you. I beg you to take me back."

"Indeed," Menahem was pacing again. "Is there anything else?"

Gomer slumped to the ground. "You have won, my lord."

23

But I will fence her in with briars and thornbushes; I'll block the road before her to make her lose her way.

Hosea 2:6

The royal sedan chair lurched toward the cramped confines of the Samarian marketplace. Gomer's usually sullen mood was slightly abated. She had convinced Menahem to take her to worship at the shrine of Ashtoreth, after hinting at the delights she could bring him in the cool shade of the high place. As promised, she had given him much pleasure there. And, as usual, their embrace was more of a battle for dominance than an act of love. *Love?* Gomer laughed sardonically to herself. *It is nothing more than a demanding hunger in Menahem that only I can satisfy.*

Gomer studied Menahem sitting beside her in the sedan. His rugged profile, his air of mastery, the exquisite nobility of his frame, his handsome features, even the way he braided his beard like his Assyrian friends—all these qualities once had mingled to excite her. But that was before she discovered the possessiveness of the man.

She suffocated under his selfish demands; and the more he took of her, the more he wanted.

As always when he was through with her, he showed no further interest. As though Gomer were not present, he stared out his side of the chair, lost in his own thoughts. Gomer often wondered what brought him back to her again and again. She sat like a captive bird in her royal trappings, awaiting the time when his urges would bring him back to her for the night. His visits were her only entertainment now. Menahem no longer took her to the gay parties and feasts of his kingdom. She feared he was tiring of her, and she spent many hours thinking of ways to hold his interest. She had the hours to spare.

Boredom and confinement. Gomer contemplated the words with contempt. *Is that not what pushed me from Hosea's arms? And now I fare no better.* She fingered her necklaces of gold from Ophir and the precious topaz of Cush upon her garments. She thought of the ornate home where she resided, and she realized these were the things that caused her to bear life with Menahem and not Hosea. Again she wished for Hosea to be more like Menahem. *Why must I choose between the love I crave and the security of wealth?* The chair halted abruptly and Gomer was thrown against Menahem. The king thrust his head out the curtain, cursing the servants who carried them.

"Forgive us, O lord, but the crowd does not permit passage," a servant said with a bow.

Gomer peered out her curtain. Her heart thumped wildly when she caught sight of a familiar figure waving his arms at an angry mob. "Hosea," she breathed without realizing she had voiced the name.

Menahem squeezed her arm. "I warn you, woman, do not think of escaping me again."

Gomer ducked behind the side curtain, but it was too late.

"Gomer!" Hosea shouted, and left his bench to come to the sedan's window. "I have prayed I would see you again."

Gomer shrank away from the window. "Go away."

"Why did you leave me, Gomer?" Hosea persisted. "I thought that was all behind us."

"He lets a woman make a fool of him publicly!" Menahem roared with laughter. "Look at the little man, on his knees before a woman," he called to the crowd, who responded by joining in his revelry.

With the laughter to disguise her words, Gomer hissed, "Stop it, Hosea. Don't let them mock you."

"I don't care about them." Hosea was still reaching up to her. "I want you home."

With Menahem goading the crowd on, the noise of their hilarity pricked Gomer's heart. "How can you let them laugh at you?"

"What is your answer, Gomer?" Hosea ignored her question. "Are you coming home with me?"

Gomer felt the pressure of Menahem's threat on her elbow. She could see the only way out of her dilemma was to convince Hosea she no longer had feelings for him. *Why must he be so stubborn?* She cursed herself for having to resort to cruelty.

Taking Menahem's arm, she spoke to Hosea. "Is it not clear to you yet? I have made the choice you set before me. I worship my king. I desire no other." Gomer nearly choked on her lies. She was dangerously close to tears as she listened to the renewed jeering from the crowd. She could not look at Hosea's face.

"I do not believe you," Hosea shouted at her.

"You heard her," Menahem scoffed. "Now, run along

home, prophet, or perhaps find yourself another harlot to grovel before."

"Beware!" Hosea's prophetic voice boomed unexpectedly through the marketplace. "She is chosen of God!" The giggling slowly subsided and was replaced with a superstitious silence. "As Israel is chosen, so is this woman. Let Israel be warned. Destruction is nearer now than when I first came to you. Wickedness will be recompensed."

Fear rippled through the crowd in hushed murmurs. An air of panic surrounded them. The people in the streets were pointing at Gomer and whispering among themselves. Before she knew what was happening the words "chosen," "cursed," and "stay away from her" were pelting her like sand in a windstorm. Even Menahem was eyeing her suspiciously.

"He is a madman!" Gomer leaned out the window of the chair and shouted to the crowd. "Would the Lord choose a harlot?"

It was as if she had not spoken. The crowd withdrew fearfully from the royal carrier, and the servants picked up the sedan chair to return to the palace. Gomer stared at the people, incredulous. "Surely you cannot believe him!" she screamed back at them. She dazedly shook her head. Menahem looked away from her. *What has Hosea done to me? I will be scorned by anyone who has sense enough to fear the gods.*

Hosea stared after the carrier until it had disappeared around a corner. Gomer's benediction of devotion to the king echoed shrilly in his ears. His heart was rent with grief. The denial of her love for him chased away all hope, and even the thread of prayer to which he had clung so long unraveled before him.

The crowd was dispersed, but a few stragglers lingered

to whisper and point at him. He overheard a toothless old man as he passed. "I've watched the family of Beeri since the old man died, and that one has always been strange," he pointed at Hosea. "Mark my word, no good will come out of that house."

Hosea stuffed his hands in his girdle and kicked savagely at the dust of the road. What did it matter what people thought of him? He had lost Gomer forever. As much as the thought stung, he could not help thinking maybe it was better to be free of her. She had caused him nothing but heartbreak.

24

When she runs after her lovers she will not catch up with them. She will search for them but not find them. . . . She is a lonely, wandering wild ass. The only friends she has are those she hires.

Hosea 2:7; 8:9

"The woman is cursed," Mara whispered to the king. She drew her cloak about her, warding off the morning chill of the palace throne room. "She caused my son's death and took my husband. Sire, my counsel is to stay far from her."

Gomer could not hear what Mara said, but the hewn stones of the floor beneath her that summoned the icy depths of the earth up into their surface were no colder than Mara's face. "She is lying to you!" Gomer cried. "Her eyes have been clouded with jealousy since my first days at the king's chapel. Liar!" She struggled against the strength of Ka'Tan's restraint as she lunged for Mara, who was perched on a bench at the foot of the throne.

"My lady, this behavior will worsen your plight," Ka'-Tan whispered coarsely into Gomer's ear. *"Please,* my lady."

Menahem watched the scene in amusement before giving attention to an ant on the arm of the throne. Idly he blocked its path. "How is it you have entered the throne room unbidden, Gomer?"

"Am I forbidden to see you, my lord? My only bidding is to seek your presence at my table this night." Gomer bowed before him. "My desire for you has caused my boldness, sire. Please, forgive me if I have caused you displeasure."

"Forgiven," the king nodded. As he listened to her groveling, contempt curled his lip and his eyes flickered. "And how is it you have concluded that I should disregard my schedule and dine with you this night?" Menahem did not look at her but continued to torment the ant, blocking its every path.

Gomer's eyes were wide. Humiliation reddened her face. "It has been so long since you came, my lord," she pleaded. A hiss, not unlike demons deriving pleasure from tormenting souls, rushed at Gomer from the host of royal attendants.

"Shall I have Jemima sent to your chambers this night as planned, sire?" Mara leaned toward the king and smiled. "Her days of preparation are completed. Keren is another fair woman who desires nothing but to give you pleasure."

"I was wise to make you keeper of the women, Mara." Menahem watched Gomer closely as he spoke. Keeping his eye trained on her, he flicked the ant away with perfect aim. "But this night I will attend to Gomer."

Gomer straightened and threw a look of triumph at Mara. Overwhelmed with victory, she turned and exited without waiting for the king's dismissal. The sound of Manahem's taunting laughter followed her out, and she remembered another time, long past. . . .

Gomer paced the veranda, wringing her finger as she twisted an emerald ring around it. The sun was glowing soft red as it rested on the rim of the western mountain range, and still Menahem had not appeared. Gomer checked the hallway again for Ka'Tan returning with news of the king's arrival. Scurrying to the polished bronze mirror, she once more inspected her amber reflection. The metallic mirror made the deep purple and gold folds of her dress appear dull and brown, but it assured her that each ornate comb creasing her hair and each necklace and jeweled band was in place. She turned before the oval mirror and smiled to see how the tunic hugged and flared seductively. It was worth the wait to be once again in Menahem's favor.

The door to her apartment opened. "What did he say?" Gomer leaned toward Ka'Tan so expectantly she looked as if she would topple.

"Matters of state have detained him."

"He is a liar! Thus he excuses himself from all unwanted invitations. I will not allow him to mock me like this." Gomer paced again.

"My lady, I made further inquiries."

Gomer stopped to give him full attention.

"I reported to his majesty how I have called upon homes of the king's favored subjects and how they have turned me away, not even allowing me entrance. He replied that the behavior of my mistress's acquaintances was not his concern."

"If it is not his concern, then why did he imprison my husband for claiming me?"

Ka'Tan cleared his throat. "I do not mean to imply that his majesty was dishonest." His eyes twinkled mischievously, and he was once again her childhood conspirator. "But I went elsewhere in the palace for answers."

"Ah, my crafty servant, *I* will give you no reproach." Gomer smiled at him. "Tell me, what plot did your slyness uncover?"

The smile left his face and he lowered his voice. "My lady, there is *indeed* a plot. Mara has been poisoning the king's mind with foul lies." Gomer's eyes narrowed as her servant spoke. "She bears witness against you, testifying to Hosea's warning that you are cursed."

"Hosea did not say *cursed,* he said *chosen.*"

Ka'Tan waved away her interruption. "She has told the king you were the cause of her losing all she held in esteem. She is pleading with him to stay far from you lest she lose her royal husband also."

"I should have guessed Mara was the cause of this."

"She is also the one responsible for turning the elite of Samaria against you with her accusations. They are afraid to have you present at their celebrations."

Gomer stared at Ka'Tan but no longer saw him. Her mind reviewed the scene at the marketplace where Hosea proclaimed her the chosen of God, and in her heart she knew it was not Mara who was responsible. Once again the Lord God had toyed with her, and Mara only used that happening to her advantage.

Ka'Tan shuffled his feet nervously. The abrupt change in her demeanor startled him. "Are you well, my lady?"

Trancelike, Gomer spoke. "Where is my wind-lover? I need him so, but he comes to me no longer. I cannot find him. Menahem was a part of him, Hosea also, but I need *him*, not a likeness."

Ka'Tan reached out and touched her shoulder softly. "Perhaps you should lie down."

Gomer suddenly saw him. "Do not try to deter me," she snarled. "Menahem will not mock me!"

Ka'Tan withdrew his hand as if flames had touched it. "Deter you from what, my lady?"

Gomer's eyes misted. "I have chased the wind away. I have offended him by accepting another in his place. I wondered why I must be forced to choose between Hosea and Menahem. My mistake was in the choosing. I stopped searching for love like Abba's and settled for a likeness. I must leave them both to find it."

"If it is love you seek, return to your husband."

"You do not even know Hosea." Gomer's eyes cleared and settled sharply on Ka'Tan.

"I have met him, and I know his love is faithful."

"It is more than faithfulness I desire. Hosea loves me only for my repentance, so he can thrust out his chest and boast that he has added me to the host of the Lord's fools. I admit, his love is near what I seek, but it is only the image seen in quiet waters."

"If you seek perfection, you will find it in no man," Ka'Tan said sagely.

Gomer looked past him. "I will keep looking. And I will find love." Her eyes flashed suddenly. "The Lord God thinks He has defeated me, but I will have vengeance. I will prove I can replace what He has stolen from me."

Ka'Tan stepped back involuntarily. His face revealed shock, and he peered closer at her. "I recognize the look in your eyes. Hate has always been there, only clothed, so that I could not detect it."

Gomer laughed caustically. "You see, even my servant cannot accept me as I truly am. I am right. There is no love here."

"No, Gomer, you are wrong. There is love here. I love you like a daughter. Hosea loves you. You are to be counted blessed for you once enjoyed the love of a father. The only place there is no love is in you. And you will not recognize the love you seek even when you find it, unless you banish the hate from your heart."

"Are you now a prophet also?" Gomer sneered at him. "Samaria seems to be overrun with them."

Ka'Tan stared as if seeing her for the first time. "These many years I have been deceived. I thought you merely a spoiled child, but you are a woman who has chosen the unalterable path of bitterness. How could I have not seen it before?"

"If I had shown you how I am, would you have been loyal to me?" Gomer's voice was laced with animosity. "Do you understand now? I am loved only for what I pretend to be. I seek one who will love *me!*" Tears coursed down her cheeks.

"Amaziah wanted me as his brazen lover, Menahem loves the sly vixen, Hosea loves the woman he thinks I would be if I repented, and you, the daughter you never had." Gomer screamed at him. "I am none of those things! I am only me. Won't anyone love just me?" she sobbed wretchedly, holding her head between her hands, and rocked back and forth.

Ka'Tan's mouth hung open. He looked at the floor shamefacedly but spoke not a word. With stooped shoulders he trod heavily out of the room.

Gomer's scarlet cloak billowed behind her as she hurried through the damp streets of Samaria. The torches burning along the road did little to light the way of a woman whose eyes were darkened with desperation. Tumultuous thoughts propelled her. *I must leave them both and find the love I lost,* she hissed to herself.

She foraged her way through a soup of filth caused by seasonal rains dripping slowly to an end. Though she had to hold her cloak high to keep the hem from the mire, she was conscious only of her destination and waded through the mud undaunted.

Her mind whirled with unsuccessful attempts to erase

the memory of the evening. One by one she had sought entrance to the feasts at wealthy homes in the city. Homes that she would not have gifted with her presence since becoming the king's consort, tonight shunned *her*. Her reproach was evident at each locked gate. Silence and fear were her only escorts.

The moon was high overhead as she numbly approached the door of the lowest hovel in the city. Obviously the outer wall had never been washed and the crumbled edges of the clay bricks revealed the inner lamplight through spacious cracks. The stench of sour wine and filth made her gag, and obscene laughter erupted through the open door. Gomer stood at the threshold, repelled by the slurred shouts that bellowed forth but compelled by despair to enter.

Initially no one noticed her presence, but her manner of dress soon attracted the leering attention of every man in the room. Gomer smiled uneasily. What if no one here would have her either? What would she prove to Hosea's God then? With the ease acquired from years of practice she swayed her limbs imperceptibly. The naked eye could detect no movement; her seduction was perceived inwardly. Since childhood Gomer had been accustomed to whispers accompanying her entries, but in these murmurings she detected the superstitious fear encountered everywhere since Hosea's denouncement. She fidgeted as the word *cursed one* assaulted her ears. Infamy branded her even among the infamous.

I cannot fail this time. She set her jaw in determination. This place is my last hope—there is nowhere left. Humiliation colored her neck and face as the men turned away from her.

"Is there an extra goblet for me?" She approached the

back of a man. His hand froze around the pitcher of wine he tilted from a trenched pouring block. A grimy handprint stained the unglazed porous pitcher as he replaced it in a hole carved into the table for that purpose. He turned further from her.

"Do not slight *me!*" Gomer grabbed the man's sleeve and jerked him around angrily until his bearded, toothless face loomed hideously before her. She retreated in fear, and laughter roared around her.

Gomer eyed them all hatefully until by her stares alone she silenced the room. Slowly she circled the tables. Each man showed her his back as she passed. One even spit in her path. With the toe of her gilded leather thong Gomer ground the saliva beneath her. *I must find someone here,* she panicked. Desperation pushed her beyond reason. *I could offer him payment to come home with me!* She weighed the idea favorably, blocking out the stupifying degradation.

Her eyes fell on a man slumped at a corner table, with his head lying on his crossed arms. She made her way toward him. Every eye followed her. Her extravagant garb fell in soft folds around the stool she sat upon and the luster of its cloth shone brighter against the dull filth of the man.

Gently she laid her hand on his sweaty back. She was certain by the way his muscles flinched at her touch that he was conscious. "I spied you from the doorway," she said, allowing her knee to rest against his leg. A musty smell arose. "I was drawn to you even from that distance." Gomer softly brushed back his dark, tousled hair and nudged his leg with her knee. He buried his face deeper in his arms.

"Do not be shy," she cooed. "If you are afraid, I have a

few gold rings that may purchase some courage." She tried to giggle at her pun, but the noise sounded more like strangling. The man's shoulders shook.

"Please." Her voice was frantic. "At least walk out the door with me. You can leave me then if you want."

The man shuddered and reluctantly raised his head. Gomer smiled in relief. At first she only noticed that his face was wet with tears, then slowly recognition entered her eyes. The face was heavily bearded and dark with grime, but the boyish mouth and gullible eyes were unmistakable. Gomer gave a sharp scream and jumped back, clasping her face with her hands.

Fresh tears washed Dan's face, causing puddles of teardrops to stain his tunic. A miserable sob ripped from his throat, and Gomer's brother laid his head once more upon his arms.

25

But you have cultivated wickedness and raised a thriving crop of sins. You have earned the full reward of trusting in a lie. . . . But it is too late! Israel has thrown away her chance with contempt, and now her enemies will chase her. . . . You may no longer stay here in this land of God; you will be carried off to . . . Assyria.

Hosea 10:13; 8:3; 9:3

"What?" Gomer murmured, her head resting listlessly against plump cushions in her courtyard. She lay each day beneath the shade of a palm branch booth, attempting to recall lost days of joy, but always, in the midst of her daydreams, a nightmarish vision of Dan obliterated them. His wretched face haunted her, and she daily grew more pallid, striving to deny the hopelessness in his eyes, striving to forget how it mirrored her own. "Forgive me, Ka'Tan, what were your words?"

"My lady." He bowed before her. "The king is here."

"He's here?" Gomer repeated incredulously. "Menahem is here?" She was suddenly attentive and raised from the cushions to straighten her garments and inspect herself. Suddenly aware of her pale complexion, she mercilessly pinched her cheeks to bring the blush of life back into them. "Where is he?"

"Awaiting you in your chambers, mistress," Ka'Tan answered.

"Ask him to wait on the veranda. I must not appear too eager." Gomer breathed deeply and smiled at the return of her good fortune. Surely the past months had been only a nightmare.

As Ka'Tan left, Gomer tilted her head back and once again peals of her raucous laughter lighted the halls. *Three moons have passed and I've been visited only by visions of my brother's eyes. The gods are changing my fortune, I feel it.* This night she would set aside her games and reveal her pleasure at the king's return. Time had served to soften her toward Menahem so that even his long absence could not anger her or detract from her longing for him.

Standing outside her open chamber door, Gomer bit her lip, composing herself before entering. She espied Menahem as he crept about strangely within the room, taking stock of her rarest jewelry and most valued possessions. He gingerly held a flimsy fabric before him and eyed it in the light filtering in from the veranda. He balanced baubles in his hands as though weighing their value and dusted a perfume jar with his index finger, while inspecting its contents.

Perhaps he desires to give me a gift and wants to be assured he will not purchase a thing I already own. Even as she thought so, her brow wrinkled with doubt. The king seemed startled when Gomer cleared her throat behind him.

Replacing the jar on her dressing table, he spoke. "Interesting scent. Nard, is it not?" Menahem's nostrils flared.

Gomer nodded. She held out her arms to him and smiled. "I knew you would come."

"Did you?" Menahem's mouth curved slightly. He remained aloof.

Gomer overlooked his distant manner. "My lord," she took hold of his arm. "Would you like to share an evening's repast and the pleasure of newly scented sheets?" Gomer gestured to her large brass bed, another gift from her king.

"What I would like is," he paused to smile at her and Gomer's anticipation mounted, ". . . some wine."

Disappointment thickened Gomer's voice. "Bring some imported wine to the roof, the white from Lebanon," she instructed Ka'Tan and looked at Menahem, raising her eyebrows in question. "Or would you prefer some spiced wine?"

Menahem smiled. "Spiced will be appreciated."

Gomer smiled also, remembering the revelry of the evening they last partook of the strong drink. "Ka'Tan," she added. "We will dine 'neath the stars this night."

"As you bid, my lady." The servant bowed and departed.

The king and his consort climbed to the roof. Gomer breathed in the evening's vibrant air, filling her lungs with its freshness. She reveled in the pleasure of reinstatement in the king's favor and looked at him, silently grateful. Leaning against the wrought iron lattice that encompassed the roof, she entwined her fingers through its openings to peer at the last rays of the setting sun. With its departure, cooler breezes swept across the roof. Samaria below was speckled with the luminescent glow of oil lamps as they lit window crevices here and there. In the upper city, the temple of Baal was clearly etched with torchlight along the steps leading to its wide porch. She

217

could feel Menahem's eyes on her, and the evening was perfect.

Contented, Gomer retired to an elegant couch lined with plump cushions, across from the king in his tall, stately chair. Gomer beamed at him as Ka'Tan brought their wine and dinner of roasted quail stuffed with parched grain, served with assorted cheeses and fruit. With such delicacies and the king's presence, she could almost forget her past suffering.

Ka'Tan placed the last dish upon the table before them, and Menahem ordered, "We do not wish to be disturbed this night." Gomer flushed with pleasure.

Ka'Tan bowed. "If you require my services, my lady, I will be in my chamber."

Gomer tried to lace the meal with enticing conversation, but Menahem remained drearily silent. At its end, Gomer raised her cup high to gain his attention and declared, "To the king's health. Long may he live," then thoroughly downed the wine in a tribute to him.

Menahem sipped from his cup and ran his finger around its rim. "Is long life how you also saluted Shema?"

The wine spewed from her mouth. "My lord?" The last bit of drink caught in her throat and she coughed. "Mara has poisoned you with lies, sire, I—"

"I did not come to discuss concubine gossip, Gomer." He moved leisurely beside her on the couch. "Pul, the Assyrian king, has asked for more tribute. Since it is my desire to keep him as an ally, I have levied a higher tax from Israel's nobility."

"But I am exempt from your taxes." Gomer leaned into the couch and pulled her skirts seductively about her legs. "What has this to do with me?"

"You are not entirely exempt. Two Assyrian soldiers

who are friends of mine have made a request for a personal gift, if you will, for their father, a struggling slave merchant." He placed his hands on her shoulders and slid the sleeves of her tunic down around her arms. "What price do you think inferior ware will bring at the market?"

"What do you speak of?" Gomer shrank from him.

Menahem stood abruptly. He leaned over her menacingly and braced his arms against the couch 'It has been rumored that you roamed Samaria's streets begging for a lover."

Gomer's eyes rounded. She sensed he was no longer playing games, and for the first time she feared his wrath. "My lord, forgive me." She knelt on the floor before him and kissed his hand. "You did not come to me as you promised, and the curse—"

"Enough!" He slapped her.

"My lord," she sobbed, covering her face.

"If you can beg a stranger, then beg *me*." His eyes took on a vicious gleam and he whispered gravely.

"I do, sire. I have already pleaded for you to share my bed. Do you not know I continually desire your presence?"

"You would lie with a dog," he hissed and twisted her hair sharply. "*Beg* me!"

"Please, sire. Please stay with me this night and I will do anything you ask. *Please.*"

"Bah," he croaked. With the heel of his hand he sent her sprawling across the roof and laughed at her. "I need not share your bed to make you do my bidding. You are no longer the wild mare I loved to harness. You are broken, Gomer." Menahem picked up the hem of her gown. "However, I know of another colt who will fill your garments nicely."

219

Gomer looked up at him and spat. "You swine."

"Did you truly believe that hiding behind my power and greatness would keep you from harm? You should have gone crawling back to the prophet while he yet desired you. He seemed to believe in your worth. I do not. You no longer excite me, Gomer, and I fear there is no mercy for those who bore the king." He clapped his hands, and Gomer found herself being forced to her feet. Before she could scream to summon Ka'Tan, a hand covered her mouth. The iron grip of two Assyrian soldiers held her.

Menahem raised his chalice and toasted the air as she was dragged, struggling, from the roof. "To the *next* mare to be snared by the king." His laughter floated from the rooftop and was absorbed by the noise of the night.

26

But . . . you broke my covenant; you refused my love. . . . My people are determined to desert me. . . . No, I will not punish you as much as my fierce anger tells me to. . . . Then the Lord said to me, "Go, and get your wife again and bring her back to you and love her, even though she loves adultery. For the Lord still loves Israel though she has turned to other gods and offered them choice gifts."

Hosea 6:7; 11:7,9; 3:1

As the quickly rising heat of the month Elul dried the dew drenched earth, the moisture was replaced with a different kind, the sweat of man's brow. Momentarily resting on the gently sloping terraces of his vineyard, Hosea straightened and wiped the perspiration from his face. Harvest held none of the usual enjoyment for him, but only bent his back with strenuous labor.

He glanced down at the branch he left unharvested. It hung heavy with fruit that trailed the ground. Though the law of God commanded he leave only the fallen grapes and corners of the field for the poor to glean, Hosea always left the lowest vines also, the ones hidden from the sun by their own leaves so they remained ripe longer. The poor ridiculed him just as the rest of Samaria, but they argued for the right of gleaning his vineyard.

He watched Arioch below him sprinkling olive oil over drying grapes, preparing them to be turned. The raisins obtained from the final harvest would be one of the few additions to the bread that would sustain them through winter. Their olive grove had been claimed in taxes. Further down, on the lowest terrace, Lois and Bilhah pranced within the wine vat. Hosea nearly smiled at the sight. *I am sure that is the closest I will ever come to seeing my sister dance.* A stinging vision of Gomer's swaying form flashed through his mind, but the mist of depression quickly fogged it.

His dulled eyes scanned the vineyard, absorbing the scene. He knew his family was concerned for his solemn behavior, but he was unable to withdraw from his inner retreat. Hopelessness covered him with a weight that defied prayer.

A leather bucket bulging with ripened grapes hung from Hosea's shoulders. In the past the weight of a full skin would have filled him with satisfaction. The vineyard kept the family of Beeri from the desolation of poverty, a fate claiming most of the citizens of Israel. But his heart was clouded now and canceled out all joy.

Hosea trudged wearily toward the vat with his pouch of grapes. The wind carried voices to him, and he glanced about for the source. A tall, black man was beside the wine vat and as Lois pointed to him, the man leapt the terraces like a swift-footed runner and stood before him.

"My lord," he panted. "Please, I need your help. They took her last night. I found out this morning. She was not in her chambers. Half of her possessions were gone. She has been sold."

Hosea stared at the man, perplexed. He seemed familiar but Hosea could not remember where he had seen him. "The grace of God be upon you, my friend." Hosea lifted his hand toward him. "You are breathless. Have some grapes to refresh yourself, and then, when you are rested, tell me the matter."

The man pushed away the cluster Hosea held out to him. "My thanks to you, but I cannot. My errand is too urgent."

"What *is* your errand?" Arioch asked, making his way around the row of vines below them.

"Please, my lords, grant me your favor. I have come seeking salvation."

"Salvation comes only from El Shaddai, but we will do what we can. You are our guest, we are your servants," Hosea assured him.

Panic left the man's eyes. "I am Ka'Tan, headservant and devoted slave of my mistress, Gomer."

"You are Gomer's servant?" Hosea's face paled.

"Yes, my lord. She has been sold to an Assyrian slave merchant. They took her last night, but I did not discover her absence till dawn. You must save her."

"Did she send you to fetch me?"

"No, my lord." Ka'Tan was impatient. "I knew not her predicament until this morning, when it was too late. But if you will come with me now, we can catch up to them. I cannot help her alone."

Hosea turned his back resolutely and ripped grapes from the vines violently. Ka'Tan threw a despairing look toward Arioch and then back at Hosea. "Surely you will not forsake her?"

There was no answer. Hosea's shoulder muscles twitched, and he plucked the grapes with such force he bruised them.

"Please, my lord! You accepted me as your guest and

vowed your protection. Would you revoke your word?"

Hosea whirled on him. His lips twisted caustically, and his icy voice reflected his heart. "Where is her wonderful king now? Let her call on *him* for help."

"But sir, *he* is the one who sold her."

Hosea's expression fell.

"You *must* help her. You are the only one!"

"No! She is finally free from the burden of her husband. It is as she wanted it." Hosea bent again and continued to reap.

"I beg you, my lord." Ka'Tan fell on his knees.

Arioch reached out and touched the servant's arm. "I am sorry. Even if my brother relented, we could not go. We have just begun the harvest. The grapes would spoil on the vines before we returned."

"But they left only this morning," Ka'Tan blurted. "We could—"

"We do not not know which way they went," Arioch interrupted. "There are highways leaving Samaria in all directions. What if we followed the wrong one?"

"But they will sell her as a *slave!*" The old servant was near tears.

"I am sorry for her," Arioch said. "But we must look after our family. We could not survive winter without wine to warm us, and the excess vines are our only means to purchase grain and a few vegetables. Who can make raisin honey from withered grapes? Surely you can see that we have no choice."

Ka'Tan looked at Hosea. The prophet's back remained firm. The servant hung his head and retreated from the field.

Hosea roamed aimlessly though the darkness. He yearned for the solace of his field, but Arioch kept watch in the tower for wild animals that might ravish the vines, protecting the fields one more night for the poor who would glean a last time. His search for solitude led him to the eastern slopes of Samaria where the damp tombs lay. But solitude was not solace, and Hosea squatted to pry absently with his fingers into the shallow topsoil of the hillside.

Hollow thumps broke the silence of the graves. Hosea turned to witness two ibex facing each other in the silvery moonlight. The younger of the wild goats, known by his smaller size, pawed the ground, steadily eyeing the elder. The larger merely stood his ground, snorting great puffs from his inflamed nostrils.

Presenting his horns, the younger goat challenged the other, prancing back and forth, emitting a short series of whistles. The smaller animal pawed again and threatened with a grunt. The elder's thick fleece rippled but he showed no further signs of retaliation. The youth advanced, but retreated quickly when there was no response from the larger goat. Again he charged and retreated, shaking his head in awed perplexity. Sweat glistened off his supple flanks, and his spongy hoofs made hollow sounds against the boulders upon which he pranced. Confusion tensed him, and he strained his neck to eye his opponent. There was no escaping the elder's stalwart stance. In surrender the young goat bucked and streaked away, defeated in a battle never fought.

The moon was bright, and its icy light frosted the abandoned hillside with a deathly pallor. The location suited Hosea's mood perfectly. As he sat considering the scene of the near battle, the face of Ka'Tan reared again before him. He closed his eyes to block it out, but the servant's cry for help reverberated in his ears. There was no escaping it, and now, here among the tombs, Hosea knew why.

I am like the young ibex, aren't I, El Shaddai? I have

exhausted myself these last three days, waging a war of hostility. And now I am battle-fatigued from fighting no one. Or is it You I am resisting? I have learned by now that I cannot long ignore Your call. Hosea looked into the heavens in resignation. *I am listening.*

The gentle sound was unmistakably God's voice. "Go, and get your wife again and bring her back to you and love her, even though she loves adultery. For the Lord still loves Israel though she has turned to other gods and offered them choice gifts."

Hosea pounded his forehead with a clenched fist. "I feared this would be your message!" he exploded. "But why? I cannot even prophesy anywhere because of the scorn she has brought upon me. The nation laughs and wonders when I will again lap at her feet as a whimpering dog."

Silence hung in the night air. "And now You will not answer me!" Hosea threw a handful of dirt at the sky. "Will You show me my heart again? Well, there is no need. I know its content. But I cannot so easily dispose of it as before. I don't want to!" Hosea waited for fire from heaven to consume him, eager for the punishment to end his pain.

Hosea, what is in your heart? Tell me, God's Spirit called to him on the wind.

Hosea's eyes widened. There was no reproach in the Lord's question. "I hate her!" he spewed. Having said it, a flood of trapped emotions were loosed. "I cannot hold my head up any longer. I am made a fool. I have done all You commanded, and still my wife casts me aside like a worn sandal. My dignity and repute among men is destroyed. That is my reward for obeying *You!*"

Hosea clasped his hand across his mouth, fearing God's swift wrath, but only a gentle breeze blew against him in response to his outburst. "Oh, my Lord, You have uncovered the wickedness of my soul. It is not Gomer I hate, it is . . ." Hosea could not say it. His mind rejected the blasphemous thought, but his heart was relieved to expel it. A floodgate opened, and the torment of past months gushed out unchecked. "I tried to love her, as You commanded, and I am only mocked. I am scorned and condemned. I am sick, El Shaddai. I am tired of humiliation. I am weak from striving. I am—"

No, Hosea, the voice of God reverberated in his soul. *I AM.*

Hosea remembered from the scrolls of Moses how God had called himself *I AM,* and he was filled with the awesomeness of the Lord. *If I am despised among men as God's servant, then how much more the One I serve?* Hosea finally understood. *How much more the loving Creator of all the earth suffers from the scorn and mockery of a world that hates him. If my heart is shredded thus, how much more my God's? If I have pleaded so long with my wife to love me, how much more endlessly does God's love beseech His bride?*

Hosea fell trembling to his knees, faint with the terrible holiness of God's presence. His hot forehead hit the wet grass. He dared not look up lest the flaming sword of God slice through him. "I can live no longer!" he cried. "I should be stoned for my complaints against You!"

Did I have Gomer stoned for her sin? the Lord asked.

Hosea lifted his shocked face to the sky. "No, You told me to marry her and love her." Hosea cocked his head to one side, trying to comprehend what the Lord was saying. "You wanted me to prove that You love Israel even though she loves other gods. But this is the same as what You said to me before. Am I to go running back to her and have her spurn me, for the rest of my life? I don't un-

227

derstand. I wooed Gomer though she was unfaithful. I courted her, and now she is gone again. Is not slavery her punishment, as Israel's captivity will be her just reward?"

Hosea, you would not leave your vineyard while the grapes were ripe for harvest lest they spoil. Will you leave Gomer to spoil?

Hosea moaned. "I am the lowest of men. In my bitterness I might have driven her forever from my heart. O El Shaddai, I cannot stand before Your holiness." Hosea covered his head in reverence and waited.

Hosea, if I chose Gomer to represent Israel, then why did I choose you?

Hosea felt as if all heaven hesitated while he breathed his answer. "To represent *You?*" The numbing truth of his words were verified in the winking stars, and he wept.

27

So I bought her back from her slavery for a couple of dollars and eight bushels of barley.

Hosea 3:2

"We await your inspection." Ka'Tan bowed before Hosea.

A haggard Hosea turned to answer him. "Whether the preparations are finished or not, we must leave." His voice was clipped with tension, and he returned to the stick drawing of an improvised map in the scattered dust of the vineyard.

"Ka'Tan, I believe this is the route we should take," Hosea explained his scratchings. The two men squatted. "I think the caravan would travel this route to ensure the highest bids, because it enters Beth-shan from the northwest by way of Dothan and Jezreel and gains much trade coming from the coast heading toward Damascus. But if we take the lesser traveled road, approaching from the southeast, we could arrive at Beth-shan sooner, though both routes are of equal distance."

"Do you think they are yet at Beth-shan, although they left four days ago?" Ka'Tan asked.

Hosea looked thoughtful. "It is possible. Beth-shan is a large trading city. But I doubt they would tarry there this long. My plan is to get to Beth-shan quickly, then try and overtake them between there and Syria. They will spend at least a day's trading at each city. Since it is late in the season, the caravan will not be making another trip until spring. They may travel even slower than that to make sure of selling all their slaves—" Hosea paused involuntarily, and both men felt renewed urgency. "I'm sure we can overtake them if we make haste."

Ka'Tan nodded.

"Now, there are barley-raisin cakes for morning meals," Lois buzzed around Arioch as he circled the packed donkeys with long strides. His face mirrored his usual irritation at Lois's mothering. "Are you listening?" Lois continued, pointing out each parcel as she talked. "There is parched grain and cuts of milk for the midday rest. There is not enough wine—after all, we only just finished harvesting—so I have sent jugs of curds to quench your thirst. There are cuts of milk for your supper also, but since there was not much packing space, nor enough time to bake properly," she threw a reprimanding glance at Hosea, "I couldn't send many loaves of bread. But if you ration yourselves and eat it only for supper it should last. Besides, you don't need anything that heavy until after the burden and heat of the day."

"Lois!" Arioch stared in exasperation. "It sounds to me as though you've sent enough food to feed the king's army. I think we can decide how to eat it without your aid."

Lois put her hands on her hips. "Well, don't pout so. I swear by the temple, you behave more like a child every year." She clucked her tongue and looked at Hosea.

Hosea stepped over to her and kissed her on the forehead, rescuing his brother from further annoyance. "We must leave now. We will return when we have found my wife."

Lois's eyes watered. "Is there nothing I can say to detain you? She is not worthy of your care, brother. She is only reaping the seed she sowed. Let her eat of it. Does the Lord God indulge your interference in His righteous judgment?"

Hosea held her chin. "Do you not yet understand? I have spent my years trying to teach Israel what I learned of God's forgiving love, and my own sister cannot see. What would be the fate of Israel if El Shaddai left us to eat of the foul seed we have sown? The Lord God delivers us out of our punishments before they utterly destroy us so we can learn from them, and turn from our wicked ways."

"Do you truly think she will repent?" Lois was cynical.

Hosea looked at her awhile before speaking. "El Shaddai does not confide such things to me."

The half-day's journey to Shechem was pleasant. A pass running between Mount Ebal on the north and Mount Gerizim on the south was partially shaded by thick foliage. Though the terrain had long since lost the burst of rainbow flora that painted it in the spring, the emerald beauty of the grass and trees still glazed the mountains. Hosea, noticing none of this, thought only that the dust crusting his feet weighted his steps and slowed his progress. The arid summer months had added to his anguish, and he was eager for the refreshing early rains.

At the well outside the walls of Shechem, Hosea left the small party and plodded ahead into the city, not stopping to quench his thirst. Arioch and Ka'Tan watched him depart without uttering a word, then they reveled in the sparkling icy waters, allowing the animals to drink and graze about freely. Hosea returned while Arioch was filling the last of their water flasks.

"Well?" Arioch questioned him.

Hosea shook his head. "Since no one has seen the caravan here, I know my presumption about which route they took is correct." He glanced at the food spread on the ground under the shade of a poplar tree and added with a frown, "We must hurry."

Ka'Tan spread his arm toward the meal. "We must eat." Hosea sighed and nodded.

It was sunset when they arrived at Tirzah. Though deteriorated from its original status as Israel's capital to a provincial town, Tirzah was still a significant city on the local highways. Situated in a luscious valley in the northern part of Mount Ephraim, the serenity of the village lured strangers to stay just one more day, but Hosea's anxiety blinded him to the town's delights.

The men slept fitfully that night and awoke weary, knowing it would take them all day to reach Beth-shan. The heat was unbearable, but Hosea would allow them to stop at midday only long enough to quench their thirst and water the donkeys. The animals rebelled at being denied the rich pasture of the mountains, but Hosea's determination surpassed their stubbornness. At day's end the hungry party entered the gates of Beth-shan.

Though the booths were closing for the night, the marketplace surged with people. Beth-shan was a valley city of importance and in times of war a stronghold, watered by the perennial Jalud stream. Situated near the junction of the Jezreel and Jordan valleys, the city intercepted a great deal of international trade. It commanded the routes south along the Jordan, north to Syria, and west to the coast of the Mediterranean. Hosea was sure the slave caravan would come through Beth-shan.

Information was scanty, but the citizens he spoke with remembered an eastbound slave master leaving a few days before. Hosea paced incessantly when they made camp that night, and aided by jackals, woke Arioch and Ka'Tan after only a few hours sleep. "If we make haste we can cross the Jordan at a nearby ford this night and rest afterwards. Come!" He urged the fatigued men to action.

Crossing the Jordan by moonlight did not serve to lessen the tension in Hosea's face. Instead he wanted to press on through the night. "Brother," Arioch spoke gently, but firmly. "Your weariness will be of no use to your wife when we reach her. And we *will* reach her." Reluctantly Hosea conceded, and the men had a few hours sleep before sunrise.

Mid-afternoon brought them to Beth-arbel. Hosea had heard rumors since the Damascus defeat that Syrians were infiltrating the northernmost cities east of the Jordan with the intent of absorbing them. Even so, the number of Syrians occupying Beth-arbel was shocking. Almost half of the inhabitants were foreign. But Hosea had no time for politics and scoured the marketplace for news of Gomer.

"Yes, I saw a slave who fits your description," a harried pottery merchant answered him. "She was being auctioned here only yesterday."

A woman veiled in expensive silks approached the pottery booth and fingered an elegantly painted jar. "Ah, what fine judgment you have," the merchant turned from Hosea. "I bring it to you from the finest craftsmen in Egypt for only—"

Hosea grabbed the man's sleeve roughly and jerked

him back. "What of the woman," he demanded. His haggard condition gave him a threateningly roguish appearance.

The merchant studied Hosea a moment and then spoke. "The slave merchant sold a few maidservants here, but the one you seek was too haughty. There was much interest in her, even though she was smitten with weakness, but a slave with such airs must be beaten excessively to be of any use. From the looks of her, she would either die from the abuse or her arrogance would make her a runaway. For the price he was asking, she did not seem worth the risk."

"When did they leave? What direction did they take?" Hosea grabbed the man's shoulders dangerously close to his neck.

"They left yesterday at sunset," the man sputtered. "Going east toward the king's highway."

Hosea released him so quickly it was nearly a shove. The potter straightened his robes and turned back to the unfinished sale, but his rich customer had gone. Hosea could hear the man cursing him until he walked out of hearing range.

The trio set out for Edrei in their prolonged pursuit. The red and yellow sands of the Transjordan desert bit at Hosea's face as they traveled against the gusty winds. Scanning the barrenness, worry creased his brow. He had not let himself think about the danger of entering eastern territory before. Officially Edrei was Israel's, but the further north they traveled the further from safety they roamed. Unlike the Assyrians, who hid their enmity behind the facade of alliance, the Syrians were outright in their hostilities. Hosea had hoped they would overtake the caravan before now.

The broiling sand magnified the afternoon sun and

shone white-hot beneath its rays. It had been two days since they had had adequate rest, and the men were growing faint. Arioch and Ka'Tan partook of parched grain as they walked, but Hosea refused the food. His eyes were trained on the trail with the penetrating intensity of the sun.

He pushed the plodding animals harder. Their laborious pace made him want to slay them there and run ahead up the mountainous incline. The sun had set and the stars were out when they finally saw the city of Edrei spread on the rocky bluff overlooking a southern fork of the Yarmuk river. The numerous tents of the slave caravan were silhouetted in the moonlight. Quickly searching out the one occupied by the caravan master, Hosea, Arioch, and Ka'Tan pushed aside the curtain door.

"What do you want?" snarled an Assyrian bent over his supper. The slave merchant spoke with a nasal whine that made Hosea flinch. His low forehead was beaded with perspiration and half hidden by the black hairs jutting out from his turban. He continued slopping food into his mouth, not bothering to look up.

"I've come about purchasing a woman slave." Hosea tried to keep the disgust out of his voice as he watched the man slobber over his bowl, hugging it with his short, hairy arms.

"I am retired for the night. I will open as usual in the morning. Come back then."

"We do not wish to tarry here another day, sir." Hosea grew impatient. "We have only just arrived, we've not even made camp, and we are in haste."

Slowly the Assyrian merchant looked at Hosea and his sunken eyes brightened with intrigue. "How is it an Israelite dog would show his face in a Syrian city?"

"Edrei is within Israel's borders!" Arioch corrected.

"Ho! But those borders are shrinking like an old wineskin." Bits of food flew from the merchant's mouth as he laughed.

Ka'Tan struck a threatening stance. Hosea stared evenly. "The only business I have with you is the purchase of a slave."

The Assyrian's half-closed eyes watched Hosea from over a long, hooked nose. Finally he grunted. "Did you have a particular one in mind?" he asked, with the obvious intention of uncovering Hosea's motives for transacting business in the dark. His mouth twitched as though delighted with his cunning.

"Why do you ask that?" Hosea played along. "I told you we have only just arrived. I have never seen your stock." Hosea paused and widened his eyes. "Aha!" he smiled. "I perceive you are a crafty businessman. Bring in your *entire* stock so that I may be sure of buying your choicest."

The merchant looked pleased with himself. As he shuffled out to get them, his feet seemed to walk three paces ahead of his slumped shoulders and perpetually nodding head. He came back in short order with the women.

"Mistress!" Ka'Tan fell to his knees at the sight of Gomer in bonds. Arioch kicked him, but it was too late.

"So . . ." The merchant's lips curled in a seedy grin, revealing a mouth full of decaying teeth. "You are the slave of my slave and have crossed into hostile land to redeem her. She must be of great value to you."

Hosea looked at Gomer. Her face revealed nothing as she stared ahead blankly. For the first time he noticed that her skin was beginning to lose the pearl-like luster of youth, and in the glaring light of the oil lamps surrounding the slave girls, it looked leathery. Even her eyes had lost their adolescent sparkle. But Hosea's love had not faded as beauty does. Looking back to the merchant he could feel his chance of regaining her slipping away.

"She is the one I want," Hosea remarked dryly. "I will give you eighteen shekels of silver." He held out his money bag.

The merchant looked at it and laughed. "Not enough," he sneered and pushed it back to Hosea.

Ka'Tan took off his ring and amulet and laid them on the table with the silver.

"She is worth twice this." The Assyrian remained firm.

"We have a mule and some barley." Hosea's voice was urgent, which only served to make the slave merchant more adamant.

"Waste no more of my time," he scoffed. "You must pay more than that to be in the bidding for this one." He poked a finger in Gomer's face. Hosea flinched but turned and left dejectedly.

"I must be alone," he told Arioch and Ka'Tan, and the two men did not see him again till dawn.

Hosea shifted his weight impatiently. The morning sun streaked across the milling crowd in front of the wooden slave platform with its slanted rays, warming the chill of a night spent under the stars in prayer.

The number of Syrians occupying Edrei was more appalling than at Beth-arbel. There were already dozens of their dome-shaped clay houses dotting the bluff. As Hosea listened to the slurred Aramaic dialect all around him, he knew it was only a matter of time until Edrei was claimed by the Syrians. He also knew this was only a foretaste of the judgments yet to come if Israel did not turn her heart back to El Shaddai.

Oh, how many times has the Lord redeemed His peo-

*ple, just as I now do my wife? How long will she remain
stiff-necked and hard-hearted?* Hosea was not sure if he
meant Israel or Gomer. The two had become so en-
meshed in his mind he could no longer separate them in
his heart.

He stomped his feet absently, positive the merchant
was auctioning the men servants first just to torment
him. He was impatient, but he knew if God had told him
to buy Gomer back, He would provide the means. He
was eager to see how El Shaddai would bring it about.

Suddenly the slave girls were lined up at the back of
the platform, and Hosea froze. His beloved was on display with five other women, completely naked. With
horror Hosea recalled the message he had delivered to his
countrymen about Israel. *Beg her to stop her harlotry, to
quit giving herself to others. If she doesn't, I will strip her
as naked as the day she was born, and cause her to waste
away and die of thirst as in a land riddled with famine
and drought.*

Hosea stared with near incomprehension as the vulgar
Assyrian pushed Gomer forward. She jerked her shoulder free from his wrenching grip. The slave merchant
slapped her. Hosea started forward but Arioch stepped
in front of him. "No, my brother," he said, looking at
Hosea meaningfully. The fury faded from Hosea's eyes,
and he relaxed his tensed muscles.

"This is my most prized slave," the merchant announced and began the bidding at a price far above Hosea's means. No one in the crowd responded.

"Come, come," the Assyrian clicked his milky tongue.
"Surely you can see she is of noble blood," he whined to
the crowd as he took hold of Gomer's chin. Gomer bit
savagely at the merchant's fingers. He slapped her again,
harder, and she fell to her knees. Hosea's face paled when

he saw the blood trickle from Gomer's mouth onto the wooden platform. Arioch put a restraining arm around his brother's shoulder.

"What good is a slave who will not even stand for inspection," jeered a man in the crowd. "Take her away!"

"You have truly said she is your prize," another man scoffed. "And you will never need part with your prize. No one with his wits about him would buy her!" There was a murmur of agreement and laughter.

The Assyrian's eyes darted in panic. "What will you give me for this girl?" He tried to ignore the hecklers. "She comes directly from the palace of the Israelite king, Menahem."

The crowd quieted at his words, but still no one ventured a bid. Hosea's eyes sparkled. *I will never cease to marvel at Your ways, El Shaddai,* he thought with a smile.

Nervously, the Assyrian merchant paced the platform. "It is true she is full of spirit, but a few lashes will remedy that. And she shows signs of intelligence. What a valuable addition to the home of the noble."

"I will give you fifteen shekels of silver and a homer and a half of barley," Hosea spoke with assurance. He could not resist offering the greedy man three shekels less than the night before, nor could he keep an amused smile from his lips.

A ripple of snickers accompanied Hosea's bid. "Did I not say a man with his wits about him would never buy her?" the last heckler roared, and the crowd roared with him. "Only an Israelite would bid such a fair price for a worthless slave."

The merchant glared at Hosea, but he snatched at the thread of a sale. "Who will give me twenty? Surely you can see she is worth *more* than twenty?"

There were no other bidders.

"Twenty shekels of silver," the wretched man beseeched. "Who will give me twenty?"

"I said fifteen shekels," Hosea's voice boomed. "Now give me what is mine."

The Assyrian's face went livid. He had been outwitted, and he looked furious. Reluctantly he authorized the deal.

"Sold."

28

And I said to her, "You must live alone for many days; do not go out with other men nor be a prostitute, and I will wait for you." . . . There I will . . . transform her Valley of Troubles into a Door of Hope . . .

Hosea 3:3; 2:15

It was a desolate camp, a black dot on the vast Syrian desert. The desolation only increased Gomer's loneliness inside the small traveling tent. No words had been spoken between husband and wife since her purchase. If Hosea were Menahem she could find a way to bring him to her to assuage her loneliness. But she could not fool her husband with games. He would whine about his love and her repentance, and she sought to delay the sickening display as long as possible. So she disdained him.

Gomer shifted the weight of her frail body and leaned against a camel saddle for support. A red and black striped saddle blanket carpeted the confined area of the booth, but the sand crept around the edges and graveled her improvised floor. Yet it *was* more comfortable than the slave caravan her *lover* had betrayed her to. The thought of Menahem created lines of pulsating hatred in her temples.

The tent flap was thrown back and Hosea entered. He looked at her steadily, silently organizing his thoughts. "We must speak."

Gomer sighed. "I expected you would come and prophesy to me."

Hosea knelt and flicked away some of the sand on the saddle blanket absently. "Gomer." He looked into her eyes. "You have foolishly spent your life. Do you not see what your unfaithfulness has brought you to? It is the Lord who has torn you, and only He can heal you."

Gomer looked startled. "So you admit that your God delights in tearing me?"

Hosea closed his eyes. "Why will you not listen? The Lord of Israel delights in tearing no one. He wants only your repent—"

"Why do you always speak of repentance to me?" Gomer interrupted. "I have done no wrong. I want only to be left alone. There is no sin in that."

Hosea watched her evenly. "If you believe that, then your longings have made you foolish."

Gomer reclined languidly against the leather saddle. "I have never sought to do wrong. What I have done was of necessity. Others have continually blocked my way. I only did what I must."

Hosea was frustrated. "You cannot keep blaming others, Gomer. You must take the blame for your own wickedness."

"A thousand thanks, but I will forfeit the credit to you," she sniffed. "You seem to covet credit for my repentance; why not my wickedness?"

"Cease!" Hosea spoke sternly. "This is not *Hounds and Jackals.* No *game* will reconcile you with El Shaddai." He wrung his hands, and the corners of his emerald eyes drooped. "It is hard for me to say these things to you, but you make it impossible when you refuse to understand."

Gomer arched her brow defensively. "If I sinned, it was only to pursue a dream."

The torrid air hung heavily between them in the shadowed tent as Hosea's expression became thoughtful. "We talked of this dream before, did we not?"

"Do you not remember? You asked me to give it up, along with all else I desire."

Suddenly curious, Hosea ignored her barbs. "Tell me of this dream, Gomer."

Gomer eyed him suspiciously but complied. "It was more of a call in the beginning. A beautiful call, like water falling gently from the rocky heights, and I was glad to answer it. It was a call that bid me dream."

Hosea looked puzzled. "What did this call bid you dream of?"

Still hesitant, Gomer answered, "Of joy. It made me excited. A gentle wind carried the promise of the love I lost when . . . " her voice faltered.

"Gomer!" Hosea grabbed her arms. "I was wrong. I asked you not to throw away my love for a dream because I thought your dream a lie, like mine. Now I understand. But a Sabbath ago El Shaddai called to me on the wind also. He excited me with the promise of love. Do you see?" He shook her shoulders. "I was wrong about your dream. It was El Shaddai who called to you on the wind, just as He did me. And He calls you still."

"Then why am I accused of wickedness when I answer?" Gomer's voice was hard.

"Because you did not answer *Him.* You rejected His call and hearkened to another. You created your own

243

god from the dream of love that El Shaddai birthed in you. And you believed another could give you what the Lord promised. But Gomer, He alone holds love. We can receive it only from Him. To settle for a substitute only deepens our craving."

"I know only that I have spent my life in search of a dream enticed by the wind. And now I find it was useless."

Hosea's voice was tender. "The dream was not enticed by the wind, but by God. If you had answered to El Shaddai instead of perverting His love with your selfish desires, you would not have found uselessness."

"It doesn't matter to me who called. It was a prank. I know that now." Gomer's ashen face, fraught with hopelessness, appeared twice her twenty-five years.

"No, it was not a prank," Hosea moaned. "The Lord truly beckoned you, and He does still, but you did not hearken. And it matters very much who called you, for who you answered to is who has led you your whole life."

"If it *was* your God who called to me," Gomer's face reflected bitterness, "why did He conceive hope in me again and again, only to crush it under the weight of His judgment? Whenever I have met this Lord of yours He has been a cruel trickster. He delights in my desolation."

Hosea's gaze was intent, as if by willing he could make her understand. "It is true the Lord conceived the hope of love in you, but it was another who crushed your hope. You rejected the Lord God for him. You sought to find your dream of love in a man. It is no wonder you could not be satisfied. My love is not enough—you must receive God's. A man is only sinew and bones. I can be only a reflection of the God I love." Hosea's heart beat faster as the lessons El Shaddai had taught him among

Samaria's tombs and the words that now issued from his mouth, joined in a marriage of insight. "I can give you only *my* love. You must go to El Shaddai for *His*."

"I cannot accept your words, Hosea." Gomer's face grew paler, but her expression harder. "I only followed a dream, and sinning, as you call it, was the only path I could find leading to it."

"Was it, Gomer? Didn't I show you another path to happiness?" Hosea's attention focused on Gomer so intensely she reverted to her old games.

"Happiness?" Gomer laughed. "Is that what you call the dull existence within your walls?"

Hosea flinched, and pain poured from his eyes. "Far be it from me to force my home upon you. I will set this tent amid our vineyard for you instead," he arched his arm in a half circle. "Perhaps this home will be more suitable."

Gomer's lips tightened. "I was closer to finding my dreams when I searched among the dogs of Samaria," she spewed.

Their eyes met and held for a long moment. "Why are we attacking one another?" Hosea asked sorrowfully. "You must listen to what I have been saying. It *is* El Shaddai who woos you with this dream of love, but you persist in following after another of your own making. You chase your dreams in the winds of thrill and mystery, ease and luxury. Righteousness is never found there. Will you come with me where love is found?"

"You sound like Amos now." Gomer avoided Hosea's direct questions. "Must life be dull to be righteous? What has God against luxury? I am condemned because riches are part of the love I seek."

Hosea looked at Gomer pathetically. "You are deceiving yourself. You pretend to seek only love, but it is luxury and stimulation that you covet above all else. Do

245

you yet believe they will bring you happiness? Isn't it this *happiness* that brought you to the slave market?"

Gomer examined the saddle blanket covering the sand at her feet. "I am weary of hearing about a God who wishes to heal wounds He inflicts Himself."

"Oh, Gomer!" Hosea wailed and threw himself before her. He clutched her hands in his. "You chose to ignore God's path, and now you blame Him for punishing you. The punishment is not to do harm, but to reveal your error, so you may correct it."

"I am not a child that I need punishing," Gomer's chin jutted.

"Yes, you are," Hosea threw her hands down. "My love for you is so great—no, don't look away. Look at me." He cupped her face firmly with both of his hands. "I love you, Gomer. It hurts me deeply to speak to you in this manner. It hurts you too, to hear it. But if I truly love you I will speak the truth so that you may repent.

"It is the same with the Lord." Hosea searched Gomer's face desperately. "Do you understand? This punishment is not your destruction, but El Shaddai has set before you a door of hope!"

Gomer did not answer. She could not. Hosea's touch weakened her as he probed the depths of her eyes. Her lips were moving softly, brushing the palms of his hands, but her words were soundless. He strained to hear. "What are you trying to say?"

Her voice came as quietly as breath. "But your God took everything from me."

"Gomer." Hosea inched closer to her. He brushed back her hair. "Listen closely. You have provoked the Lord bitterly. You have boasted, 'I am so rich, and I have gotten it all by myself!' But riches won't pay for your sins.

You don't realize that all you had came from God. He gave you the gold and silver you used in worshiping Baal. But now God has taken it all back—your vineyards and orchards, gifts from your lovers, the wine and clothes—all of it. He has put an end to your parties, holidays, and feasts in hopes that without all of His blessings you will have no one but Him and you will call on Him."

Gomer struggled to tear her gaze from Hosea's. *I must get away from him! As long as he holds me I am powerless.* She formed her words carefully to wound Hosea. "On bended knee is an apt place for you. Why don't you plead with me as before to return to you? Or do you need a crowded marketplace in order to perform?"

Hosea stared at her. *Now she scorns my tenderness! Is there no end to her abuses?* Through tight lips Hosea responded. "Sometimes one must plead to correct, and the wise will listen gratefully."

"Gratefully?" Gomer spat, relieved to have diverted Hosea from his preaching. "I see now why you have come to my aid. Will my gratitude satisfy some pious need of yours? Why, even Menahem had more interesting motives for pursuing me."

Hosea stood before her and roared. "Why do you goad me so, woman? It is impossible to talk with you. I bare my love to you and still you strip me with your cruelty. Do you think I plead with you because I am less a man than Menahem? I plead as the Lord God is pleading with His people, and they abuse Him just as you do me! If it is Menahem you desire I can comply. I am as much a man, Gomer," Hosea raised his arm as if to strike her, "and I can be like him if it will satisfy you."

Gomer recoiled from Hosea's dark fury. He strutted arrogantly in imitation of the king and pointed a finger in her face. "You have pushed the Lord far enough," he thundered, "and there is but one thing that can save you from His wrath."

"Repentance?" Gomer meant the word to mock him, but it surfaced with a croak.

Hosea stopped pacing midstep and his countenance lighted with hope. "Yes, Gomer, yes," he raised his arms in jubilation and then grabbed Gomer and pressed her to him. "Oh, that we might know the Lord together. Let us press on to know Him. He will respond to you as surely as the coming of the dawn, as surely as I respond to you." Hosea kissed his wife passionately. "Will you know my God?" he asked her with reverence.

Yes! Gomer wanted to shout but held her tongue. Hosea's face was close to hers, beaming in anticipation. *How I yearn to surrender.* She closed her eyes momentarily to his pleading. *It would be so easy to say yes to all he requests, to settle for the love he speaks of. But would I be responding to Hosea's God or Hosea's persuasiveness? Is this another trick? Will I believe only to be dashed to pieces, this time never to recover?*

She looked up into Hosea's expectant face. "I don't know your God. I am afraid to."

"My little one, there is nothing to fear. New birth is offered you, but you are like a child resisting in the womb. How stubborn you are. How foolish." His lips were still near hers, his arms still around her.

"Let go of your own dreams of what love should be," Hosea crooned gently. "El Shaddai will refresh you like the dew from heaven. You will blossom as the lily and root deeply in the soil like cedars of Lebanon. The Lord will continually water your . . . " he paused and caressed her cheek, "*our* garden. El Shaddai will be like an evergreen tree, yielding His fruit to us forever. His mercies will never fail."

Joy washed over Gomer like the cool waters of the Jordan. She could not remember feeling so loved since her father had held her in his arms. *The father that the Lord took from you.* The thought seemed to come from nowhere, stinging her with vile bitterness. *No matter how convincing my husband is, his God is still the same who left me fatherless and has stolen from me every gain I acquired.* She stiffened in Hosea's arms. "I am sorry, Hosea. I cannot know your God."

Hosea stared at her with disbelieving eyes as she withdrew and faced the tent wall. Waves of grief paralyzed him. His arms hung limp. His voice was husky, and he spoke as if in a trance. "How well I remember those first delightful days when I led you through the streets to my home. I had a dream then too. I told you of it before, but do you know what *my* dream was? Of a meek and devoted wife who would cherish me as I did her. But that dream was a lie that kept me from you. El Shaddai had another one. He bade me relinquish my own and chase after His. My obedience led me to you, and I was glad. How refreshing was your love. How satisfying, like the early figs of summer in their first season. But then you deserted me."

Shocked, Gomer swung around to face him.

"You broke our covenant and refused my love. It is not the Lord who has torn *me*, Gomer. It is *you.*" Hosea's voice caught in his throat.

Gomer could only stare at her husband.

"I have loved you, you and no other. I sought you faithfully when you ran from me. And you have rewarded me with adultery," he choked on the word. "You have kicked me like a dog in the streets. You have not even given me the table scraps of your love. Do you think I feel no pain? Love is a pain you have protected yourself from, Gomer. And you cannot receive love until you share with El Shaddai the suffering of giving it."

Gomer opened her mouth but nothing came out.

"You deserted me twice, and now you cast me aside again. I will not die from the pain. I will learn and grow from it. But woe is the day when El Shaddai deserts *you*. And He will, Gomer, if you keep rejecting Him. He will not strive with you forever."

Gomer found her voice. Bitterness shot like flaming arrows from her eyes. "You say your God longs for me to come to Him? Then I will answer Him just as He answered *my* longings for my father!"

29

But the east wind—a wind of the Lord from the desert
—will blow hard . . . . Therefore, a mighty wind shall sweep
them away . . . . For now is the time to seek the Lord, that he
may come and shower salvation upon you . . . For in you
alone, O Lord, the fatherless find mercy.

Hosea 13:15; 4:19; 10:12; 14:3

Gomer sat upon the clouds of heaven. She proudly
surveyed the glittering beauty surrounding her and was
pleased. Members of the royal court worshiped before
her and lay gifts of precious jewels at her feet. With godly
magic she wove the jewels into a rainbow crown and
decked herself with it.

"Queen Anath." A man not unlike Shema knelt before
her, and somehow from a distant vantage she knew she
was the queen he called to. "May we sit at your feet and
listen to your great wisdom?"

"Wisdom?" Her lips stretched into a sullen line. "My
son, I have no wisdom. Did you intend to say 'beauty' or
do you mock me?"

"But, my lady," the man continued. "Did not our lord
Baal depart two moons ago to hunt for the storehouse

where the treasured wisdom is kept? Great queen, we must seek after him."

"Let him be," Gomer pouted. "The wisdom he seeks is not something I desire. The treasure I seek is love."

"But, my lady," the man laughed, "all heaven adores you." Gomer's mother and Dan appeared at the man's side. Ka'Tan, Hosea, and her children stood behind them. Their voices echoed, "All heaven adores you." The man shrugged his shoulders, and his tone was sarcastic. "Do you not own all the love that wealth can purchase?"

"Silence!" Gomer's voice thundered throughout heaven, destroying its inhabitants, and the sound created a sirocco, like the dreaded, hot desert winds upon Israel far below. The force of the wind created a column of dust about her. She was caught within it and carried far upon its wings. Terror overwhelmed her as she turned and glimpsed the face of the Lord God. His eyes were tight slits, framed by one frenzied, v-shaped eyebrow. His cheeks were twin mountains blowing His mouth into the shape of an angry volcano spewing fire and brimstone. She sought a means to flee from Him, but the force of His breath hurled her beyond the highest heaven and into the blackness of eternity. She heard voices as of many waters hissing at her, and they cheerfully clapped their hands when there was not found a place for her in the universe.

Gomer bolted upright from her pallet and screamed into the night. Ka'Tan was quickly at her side. "My lady, what is it?"

"Make haste. Light the lamp." Gomer shook and pulled blankets up about her neck. When her servant trimmed the wick, she glanced about fearfully at the dancing shadows upon the tent walls.

"It is the fever, mistress. The water abroad will cause much illness."

"It is not the water." Her teeth rattled with irritation and fear. "It is the Lord God. He seeks to destroy me."

"Allow me to call for your husband." Ka'Tan turned toward the opening in the tent. "He is wise in the way of the Lord."

"No!" she pierced the air with a sharp scream. *He will mock me*, she thought, remembering her dream. *He has always mocked me. I understand now. He has saved me to destroy me. Perhaps even Ka'Tan has a role in this. I can trust no one.* She said aloud, "You may leave."

Ka'Tan ducked under the opening of the tent, leaving her alone with her thoughts. She shivered. *There are many paths and means leading to my destruction. Somehow, I must flee from God's wrath. But Hosea lies in wait for me to set foot outside this tent so he can accuse me of seeking lovers.*

The break of day found Gomer pacing within the tent. As the sun rose she wore a deep rut into the dirt floor. The heat assaulted the sides of the tent and radiated through her. Still she paced, nearly stumbling over a three-legged stool, one of the few provisions Gomer allowed from the house. Her pride would not permit the dark confines of the tent to be cluttered with luxuries, or even food, for which she would have to be grateful to Hosea. The only other furnishings were a rolled mat stuffed into one corner and an oil lamp.

"My lady Gomer," Ka'Tan called to her from outside the tent.

"What is it?"

"I have come with a palm branch to fan the air and comfort you." Though he seemed concerned and friendly, Gomer was wary. Deciding the refreshment he offered seemed harmless, she allowed him entrance, and he fanned while she continued to pace.

"My lady," Ka'Tan sighed as he wiped the sweat from his brow. "We must leave this tent before the midday sun consumes us with its heat."

Gomer looked at him askance. *He thinks to lure me to Hosea.* "I'll not go to him," Gomer's chin jutted forward, confusing Ka'Tan with her answer. "That is my final . . ." She swooned in the feverish heat.

Ka'Tan assisted her to the stool. Quickly reviving, she pushed him away. "Mistress Gomer." He cocked his head with concern but remained at a safe distance. "Will you listen to my reasoning? Your health requires greater care than this tent will afford. Besides, has it not been a full six sabbaths since you have seen Hosea? And what of your children? Have you no desire to see them?"

"I understand your motives. Your concern is not for my health but only to goad me into their arms. Why must I be the one removed? No one has barred *them* from this tent." Gomer remained cold.

Ka'Tan ventured further. "Jezreel and Ammi have been inquiring about you. Jezreel is now ten harvests grown, and little Ammi, why he is seven! Shall I send for them?"

"I will be here if they come," Gomer answered flatly, and was surprised how her heart felt less burdened at such a small bit of information about her sons. She decided she liked Lo-ammi's new name.

Bilhah appeared at the door. She pulled back the tent's flap, flooding the room with harsh sunlight, and peered cautiously at Gomer. "Your morning meal, mistress." She presented a basket of rolls and a smile. The warm bread smelled doughy-sweet from the sun's added baking during its journey through the vineyard, and the odor threatened to revive her. "Mistress Lois prepared them especially for you," Bilhah nodded to the bread. "It is her desire for you to know she bears no ill will."

Gomer snatched a roll from the basket and in one quick motion tossed it to Ka'Tan. "Be certain they contain no poison," she quipped impudently.

Ka'Tan's face expressed his impatience, but he said, "As you wish," then motioned for Bilhah to follow him out. By their shadows against the tent's wall Gomer knew they stationed themselves nearby. Certain they spoke of her, she strained to understand their garbled voices but could not.

Ka'Tan finally returned. "If you had not sworn loyalty," Gomer spoke, and the inflection of her voice rose with suspicion, "I would suppose you to be conspiring against me."

Ka'Tan's demeanor slumped with the injury of offense. He shook his head sadly. "Will you dismiss *me* from your life also?" Before she could reply, he bowed and left.

She threw the basket of rolls after him, but they bounced off the tent flap and hurled themselves back at her, landing in the dirt near her feet. "Why must you always play the sage?" she screamed after him.

Gomer unrolled her pallet and flung herself down, childishly ramming her fists into it. "Is there no one I can trust to call friend?" Rolling upon her back, she stared a long while at the tent ceiling and bit her lip in an effort to conceal the turmoil within, even from herself.

"Mamma?" The child's voice startled Gomer. She sat up quickly and watched Jezreel steer Ammi into the tent's interior.

"So, you have come." Gomer's voice sounded ominous even to her own ears.

Jezreel gulped and stood straighter, facing his mother squarely. "Ammi asked to see you, but perhaps we should leave. Come, Ammi," he gently pulled his brother's arm. Ammi remained before her sniffling.

"Wait," Gomer called. "I . . . I . . . you may stay for a time."

Ammi jerked away from his brother's grip and bounced from the pallet into Gomer's lap. His hopeful eyes looked into Gomer's. She painfully recalled how she had withheld her love from him and placed an arm across his back to keep him from toppling.

"Oh, Ammi," Gomer whispered. "Are only the young so swift to love?"

Little Ammi responded with a squeeze to her neck and delighted her with a kiss. Smiling, he turned to his brother. "May we go back to Mamma now?"

Jezreel looked quickly at Gomer and saw their mother's arms suddenly hang limp at her sides. "You mean *Aunt Lois*, Ammi."

"Mistress Gomer." Ka'Tan stood in the entrance of the tent and spoke to her back as she sat staring at the walls. "I must speak." When she did not answer, he boldly continued. "Hosea has taught me of his God."

Gomer turned on him in threat. "And?"

"I have chosen to follow the Lord God of Israel."

"No, you may not," Gomer bared her forearm and screeched. "I forbid it."

"My lady," his voice was tender. "You cannot prevent it."

Gomer stared at him, her nostrils flaring. Finally she spoke, and her voice challenged him. "And how have *you* profited from your service to this deceitful God?"

"If my lady will permit me to speak on His behalf,"

Ka'Tan's countenance glowed with excitement, "I will tell how He has imparted His great love to me."

Gomer rolled her eyes and crossed her arms. "What is it about this God that sets men a-quiver? I must learn His secret."

Ka'Tan ignored her. "Mistress Gomer, you alone have not fought bitterness. Long ago I was stolen from the bosom of my family by the people God calls His. I hated Israel. I searched everyplace for release from the bondage of my feelings, but there was none. Everyplace but to the most high God. I was too preoccupied with my hatred to notice that He longed to soothe my bitter heart. Thus I wounded God's heart, as you have, my lady."

Gomer held her head high. "That is what I intended to do."

"And now that you have succeeded, have you found satisfaction?" Ka'Tan sat on the ground before her. "My lady, forgive my boldness, but if God did not care about you, could you have hurt Him?"

Gomer leaned forward, bracing her arms on the stool, and drew from the strength of her hatred. "The only love I have found has been given to me from those who seek me for their own selfish purposes."

Ka'Tan sat calmly, deliberately studying her before speaking. "I have considered your justification, my lady, but truly I do not understand how you can reject God on that basis. *All* earthly love is selfish."

Gomer seemed to cast her focus afar. Ka'Tan's reasoning pierced like an arrow to deflate her bitterness.

"Mistress," Ka'Tan spoke softly. "Permit me to advise you. You must give yourself to God and accept His love."

Gomer rose from her stool and whirled on him. "No, I would be destroyed!"

"The way *you* have destroyed those who offer you

love?" Ka'Tan raised his eyebrows. "My lady, you have not given, you have not even taken love."

Gomer pointed a finger at him. "I have taken, just as the God of Israel took Abba!"

Ka'Tan grew exasperated. He stood and placed his hands on his hips. "You took your children's mother away from them. Is that not what you accuse the Lord God of doing with your father? But you see no evil in *your* action, only God's. You would rather believe that He is filled with wrath and vengeance. If so, then what are you filled with? Gomer, you do not know Him at all."

Gomer leaned toward him, threatening, "If He is so loving, why did He take Abba?"

Ka'Tan sighed. "Why was I stolen from my family? Will you ever know? Your father was the Lord's to give and His to take away."

Gomer grimaced. "Give? What did God ever give me?"

"My lady," Ka'Tan said softly with a smile. "He gave you Hosea."

Gomer held her gurgling stomach and grimaced. She was ready to call for her servant to bring nourishment when she heard a noise. "Ka'Tan?"

A voice like that of growling gave warning of imminent danger, but Gomer was too weak to flee.

"I will not enter! I would rather see death than her!"

Ka'Tan dragged a young girl of about nine summers through the tent opening. The girl's long, black curls tossed in the air as she kicked and scratched and bit at him. Ka'Tan held her arms behind her back, and the girl's beastly black eyes penetrated Gomer.

"Lo-ruhamah," Gomer whispered her name.

The girl wrenched herself free from Ka'Tan. "I am called Ruhamah now. I am amazed you remember that much of my name. I will never forget yours."

The words were not sweet, and Gomer could not mistake the bitterness that birthed them. She stared at her daughter and felt as though she were looking into a polished brass mirror at her own, younger, reflection. She crossed her arms. "Why have you come?"

Ruhamah's eyes flashed. "The choice was not mine."

Gomer flung her arm toward the tent door and shouted bitterly, "Then leave. I indulge no tradition that demands you pay homage to your mother."

"*Mother?*" the girl laughed caustically, and Gomer cringed. "I have no mother. As for my father, who can be certain of the true one?"

Gomer drew in her breath and struck a sharp blow across her daughter's face.

Ruhamah staggered, then touched her throbbing cheek as a sly smile appeared on her lips. "So you *feel* pain as well as cause it. It will not be so hard to fulfill my vow as I feared. For years I prayed I had never been born than to be nursed at your unyielding breasts. But since I survived your dark womb, you have given me a reason to live." She assumed a bold stance and pointed a finger at Gomer. Her eyes lit with a fire from the pit of hell. "I have vowed to repay you for the pain you caused me and my family!"

Gomer's arms waved about wildly. "You mock me! You mock me!"

Ruhamah laughed at her and left.

The hot desert wind penetrated the sides of the tent and intensified the heat that blasted against Gomer. Still she trembled. She gathered her cloak tightly at her throat. Listening to the howling wind gain in might, terror struck her. *My dream! The Lord God of Israel is come to destroy me!*

When the wind whistled about her ears, she knew she must escape the threat the tent posed should it collapse under the storm's strength. She ran out with her head half hidden beneath her cloak. The arid wind whipped at her sharply, rippling the garment and slinging her hair across her face. Another fear gripped Gomer. She had not been outside the tent since arriving back at Samaria. She was unused to the open air, and all that was friendly or familiar was hidden by the sand-filled winds. She mustered strength to call on the only one she had ever sought in her trouble.

Hearken unto me! Her thoughts summoned her illusory wind-lover. *I perish! Why do you not save me? Are you but vanity as Hosea claimed?* As if in answer, the wind grew more violent. Trees doubled over as though being utilized as catapults for titans. A sound of rushing, mighty wind swirled around her, creating a fierce column of dust that obstructed her path. Its strength pushed her onward, and she envisioned herself being flung against a rock and dashed to death. She scowled at the wind and shouted, displaying the only means of defense she knew. "Destroy me, Lord! I know You long to make a byword of my name. Be swift. Am I not but a symbol of stiff-necked Israel in Your eyes? Destroy me as a warning to Your people! You care not for me!"

The intensified storm wind propelled her farther. Bits of sand pelted her so mercilessly that she had to cover her face with her hands. Through small slits between her fingers she searched for the ground beneath her, but it seemed to have vanished. All about her was vaporous, as though she walked on clouds. *Is this the edge of eternity?*

she wondered. *Is there after all no place to be found for me?*

Through a gap in the dust cloud a terrace wall with stones piled chest high appeared before her, and she knew her fear of death would be realized. Her forehead and palms dripped with sweat as she struggled unsuccessfully against the destructive force of the wind. Holding her quivering midsection, she groaned into the wailing tempest and accused her wind-lover of neglect. *So this is to be my end. Am I to be smitten by the Lord before your eyes? Why do you hide your face from me?* She shook her fist in the direction she assumed the sky to be. *You have betrayed me into the hand of God. I have been a fool to believe you could defeat Him. You have profited me nothing.*

She sliced at the air with her arm just as the tempest seemed to gather all power from the four winds at the corners of the earth. Forced to her knees, she cried to her wind-lover one last time. "Why did you forsake me?"

As the full force of the wind pummeled against her, and she braced for the strike that would surely propel her against the rock wall, the storm subsided. Gomer opened her eyes warily. Her fear was cast aside when she found she had been spared. She slumped in the dust and leaned her head against the wall to catch her breath, uncertain whether to trust the calmer air about her. Aloud she questioned. "Where are You, Lord God? Why did You not strike me?"

The wind continued to whip about her in harmless eddies and reminded her of the same gentle breeze she recognized as the call of her wind-lover. Involuntarily Gomer giggled.

"El Shaddai?" Even before she whispered His name, she knew who it was that called her and that His call would make her glad. A puff of wind blew back her hair with a caress before it passed on, and she recalled her words to Hosea that it didn't matter who called. She sensed a presence.

"El Shaddai?" she asked with diminishing distress and increasing wonder. The wind remained calm, but the lingering warmth of its touch seemed to wrap her in a swaddling band of comfort. "Perhaps I am a fool." She stood up and dusted her clothes off before challenging, "Are You who Hosea claims You to be? If so, reveal to me Your love."

There was silence. Following the path of the storm with her eyes, Gomer watched particles of dust floating in the wake of the whirlwind, and through them, as through a dark, molten glass, Gomer recognized the searching form of Hosea as he called to her on the wind.

Epilogue

Then I will cure you of idolatry and faithlessness, and my love will know no bounds. . . . In that coming day, says the Lord, she will call me "My Husband" instead of "My Master." I will betroth you to me in faithfulness and love, and you will really know me then as you never have before.

Hosea 14:4; 2:16; 2:20

Hosea stepped from the flat bottom of his master's private ship onto the wharves of northern Babylon. He left the mooring of the ship to the able crew of his master, Nusku-adad, and stood for a moment to marvel anew at Babylon's world-renowned piers and canals. They were sporadically dotted with small basket-shaped boats, bobbing tranquilly amid the activity of the wharves. Nowhere along the length of the Euphrates, which Hosea continually traveled for his master, was there such expansive business conducted as here at the wharves of Kâ rum. Hosea thought that Babylon was the only city whose main commerce took place not at the market within the city walls but at its docks. *Surely* such a city is capable of taking its independence from Assyria as it threatened to do.

Hosea eyed the superior glory of the famed wooden bridge spanning the majestic Euphrates on its five stone piers. The bridge itself seemed to announce the kingdom's intention of world dominance. Many times during Hosea's two years of captivity he had embarked on these trips for the ecentric Nusku-adad, royal ambassador for Sargon II, Assyria's king. Hosea was eager to comply; it gave him opportunity to search for his family. The exile had not been hard on him and he wished he could somehow let them know that he had not been made weak and old by captivity at forty-two.

Assyria's king, Sargon, had the custom of separating concentrations of resentful captives, squelching any chance of uprising. Two years before he had exiled Israel in this manner also, reducing them to slavery throughout his growing kingdom. Though most of Israel's captives were kept near Lake Urmia in the uttermost northeast recesses and the Guzanu province in the heart of the Assyrian empire, nearly any place Hosea traveled might well be the residence of one of his family. In two years he had found word of only Ka'Tan. The servant had not survived the Assyrian siege. Hosea's thoughts seemed always involved in his search.

"Do not waste your efforts at Zarubaba's shop on the wharves," Hosea remembered the instructions of his master, "But go directly to his home on the outskirts of the city, near the east wall. There he keeps his finest tapestries, set aside for his distinguished customers." The rough clay tablet identifying Hosea as a slave chafed his throat, and he pulled at the sweating leather round his neck to loosen the tension as he made his way past the whirl of business transactions along the wharves.

Turning onto Processional Way, the only land entrance into Babylon, the prophet gazed at the most extravagantly constructed gateway he had ever seen. The architecture was impressive, but Hosea was reminded of the warnings God had given Israel against such senseless waste when the poor within the walls were starving. *The extravagance of Babylon makes Israel's as nothing in comparison,* Hosea thought, entering the city. *It causes me to wonder how much harsher will be their judgment than ours.*

As he walked, Hosea's thoughts drifted back to Israel's day of judgment shortly after Sargon's enthronement, when Assyrian soldiers finally penetrated Samaria's walls. After a three-year siege of rationing food and water, enduring starvation, and suffering outbreaks of cannibalism, the walls fell. It seemed to Hosea the defeat came long before, when Israel spurned God's love. But the day God had warned of for nearly a century surpassed all imaginable horror.

The sky was darkened with smoke. Fire licked at those who cowered in concealment, sending them running aflame into streets puddled with blood and the waiting arms of their captors. Men resisting were brought to their knees to stare up at Assyrian soldiers who gouged their eyes with the spear. Amid forests of impaled men and petrifying screams wrought by inhuman tortures, Gomer, Lois, Ruhamah, and the women of Israel were forced to watch the disgrace of their men being led away by rings through their noses. Hosea thought of the twelve years Gomer had devoted to him and their children before the fall. Only twelve of her thirty-nine years had been lived in obedience to God. *Oh, Gomer!* Sadness overwhelmed him. *Was your dedication to the Lord only temporary? Will this new grief cause you to again blame El Shaddai and dismiss His love?*

Hosea's attention was summoned by a blast of trumpets. Turning to investigate, a gust of sand-filled wind stung his eyes. The Babylonian king, Merodach-baladan, also called Marduk-apaliddin, after Marduk, the patron god of Babylonia, was returning to the city with his royal train. *I wonder what this king would say should he discover Sargon had full knowledge of the intent of this tour?* thought Hosea.

Merodach-baladan had reigned insurgently under Assyria since Sargon overtook the province of Arrapkha nine years before. Now he returned from what he claimed as "diplomatic homage" to the ill king of Judah and the neighboring Elamite king. Hosea had heard his master speak rumors of this king's attempt to recruit these countries as allies against Sargon. *Would Judah suffer the same fate as Israel?* Hosea wondered.

He watched with interest as Merodach-baladan approached. His chariot was overlaid in gold with the silver, crowned dragon of the god Marduk in bas-relief on its sides. The stout king was ablaze with splendor. He held a golden scepter in his chubby left hand. His cone-shaped crown met his oiled and braided beard at each temple, bedecking his face with a glistening oval frame. The bodice of his robe was embroidered with star-shaped disks and from a chain round his neck hung a circular medallion bearing the sign of a star. The tunic crossed his chest from his left shoulder, draped to the opposite side, and was clasped at the waist with a like medallion.

In contrast to the awe and respect the king obviously expected, Hosea harbored pity for him. *What fate but destruction can await one who so flagrantly defies El Shaddai's laws?* Choking on the dust left in the path of the royal train, Hosea resumed his journey to the merchant's home.

At the center of the city he passed humble thatched and mud brick dwellings shaped like circular vaults. The houses were huddled close together. Their walls cast long shadows along the uneven surface of the city's narrow streets, causing midday to seem as sunset. As his eyes adjusted to the darkness, he could make out little altars set in the recesses of outer walls, reserved for carved gods. Eerie statues of deities such as Marduk, Enlil, Shamash, and even nameless genies watched his progress from their mini-temples.

Passing through the bustling bazaar, Hosea caught sight of onion-shaped domes atop yellow-glazed houses belonging to wealthier citizens, shining as embers in the broad rays of the sun. He admired the foreign architecture. The homes he now passed on the eastern outskirts were shaped like over-turned bowls set on great columns, far enough apart to allow gardens and colonnades to adorn them. He had arrived at his destination.

His greeting was answered by a huge, dark-skinned doorservant reminiscent of Ka'Tan. A familiar grief stabbed Hosea. As usual everyone he met reminded him of his missing household. "I am sent by my master, Nusku-adad, to inquire of Zarubaba concerning his fine tapestries. I am authorized to purchase some of his stock," Hosea told him.

The doorservant grunted and disappeared. Inside the gate Hosea glimpsed an adjoining garden, canopied by acacia trellises alive with lush greenery, separated only enough to allow wavering sunlight on potted plants and trees among tiled pathways.

"Good day, sir." A young woman's voice startled him as he peered through the gate to get a better view of the elegant garden. "Your master is a man of discerning taste to have chosen from my father's selection of carpets.

Please join me," the young lady motioned him toward the garden's fountain.

Hosea was grateful when she turned and walked away briskly. He had also been caught gaping at *her*. The girl's dark, sparkling eyes and assured manner fostered thoughts of how Gomer might have looked had she never known the weight of bitterness. Hosea had to swallow back tears to think how like his daughter she looked.

"Are you coming?" the girl turned to ask. Hosea hastened to her side beneath the shade of the trellises. "I am Zarubaba's daughter. In his absence I conduct his trade. What may I show you?"

Hosea found his tongue. "My master has sent me to look over the selected pieces kept at your home. He has heard of their great value."

The girl smiled. "I am pleased that word has spread as far as . . . " she glanced at the tablet around Hosea's neck, "Assyria," she finished.

"Indeed it has," Hosea bowed respectfully. "I am sent these many days through the waters with no other purpose than to purchase one of your father's tapestries."

"Every thread is wrought with the most excellent craftsmanship available. Kings and princes of many countries, including Assyria, come to my father for them," she said as she clapped her hands for a servant to bring some samples. After inspecting them, Hosea looked at the girl appreciatively. "Although I have heard talk of the beauty of these carpets, I did not expect such exquisiteness. Words fail me."

The girl laughed. "It is truly refreshing to deal with an honest man. Most customers pick at loose threads and complain the workmanship is not what they expected. All the while their greedy eyes shine in anticipation of hanging the tapestry proudly on their inner walls."

"Ah, my lost Gomer would appreciate the beauty of their design. There is no higher honor I can bestow on the work of your father's hand."

"Gomer, the Israelite slave?" the girl echoed quizically, but Hosea was lost in thoughts of his wife. *How I long for her! If only I could know that she has kept her love for El Shaddai. If only she has remained true.*

Hosea tensed, suddenly alert. Maybe it was the nearly indiscernible aroma of cinnamon that caused him to straighten and glance about the garden, or perhaps an inner knowing, but when an unmistakable throaty laugh echoed through an open window, Hosea jumped to his feet.

"Where does that window lead?" he demanded most disrespectfully.

The merchant's daughter smiled. "To the kitchen where the cooks are. Come, I will take you there to see whatever caused you such distress." Her eyes sparkled.

Hosea's heart pounded relentlessly as they rambled through a maze of corridors and inner courtyards before rounding a corner that brought them outside a closed door. The young girl put a finger to her mouth, as much to suppress her own glee as to shush Hosea. She cracked the door slightly to allow Hosea to see inside.

Fine age lines framed Hosea's eyes as he squinted to see inside the dark room. Absently he combed tufts of unruly, graying hair back with his fingers. Through the small opening he could barely see the faces of three young Israelite maidservants as they knelt at separate kneading troughs. They each wore necklaces bearing a pomegranate, the emblem of Zarubaba's household, and rough woolen garments. They looked intently into the face of an older woman who sat at a table beside them. Hosea craned his neck to see her.

The woman wore a linen tunic that draped the tops of her ankles and a woolen cloak over it. *Gomer!* Hosea's heart leapt at the sight of her, but he remained hidden. One of her arms was supported by a walking stick with a carved pomegranate atop. It was obvious from a slight twist of her sandaled foot that she had incurred some injury. Perhaps that was why she was made a cook, a task that did not require much movement. Hosea thought back to the day Gomer had tried to make bread in his sister's absence and almost laughed. Hosea winced as he noticed the same pomegranate carved permanently on her hand. Her usually shining oiled hair was dull and limp now. Captivity had been hard on her, but she was as beautiful to him as the day he had first beheld her through the veil, though her dark eyes drooped with lines of strain.

"Would that I had one to talk with me when I was young and foolish, as I have so done with you," Gomer spoke affectionately to the young maidens as she pondered the lack of female companionship in her life.

"But have you not had the guidance of which you speak?" one of the girls questioned. "It is known far and wide how the prophet beseeched you."

"You misunderstand. I spoke only of my desire for friendship. I wasted my youth seeking to be rid of companionship, including that of my husband's. But I long to have those years restored to me." Gomer's eyes drooped further.

"Do you not fear for your husband?" asked another of the maidservants, whose eyes revealed obvious longing for her own husband.

Gomer sighed in affirmation. "And his family and our precious children. Our daughter and sons have been separated from their own families also. Israel's punishment is hard, but it is just."

Anguish exuded from the servant girl's face as she queried, "But do you not sometimes blame the Lord God in your heart for this separation from our families and country?"

Gomer answered with loving patience. "Is a parent to blame for taking the rod to a rebellious child? If God willed it, Israel would now be but dust in the wind. I know the truth of what I speak. I have seen God's power in His love. Rightly you have said," Gomer nodded to the first girl who spoke, "that my husband beseeched me. And I finally responded to him. But he is only a man. There was a day when I responded to God and called Him 'Master,' but now He is more." The adoration in the flecks of her dark eyes spoke of how much more.

A sudden gust of wind blew open the door, calling Gomer's attention to Hosea, waiting in the threshold. His eyes shone like emeralds at dawn, breathtaking in their brilliance. The breeze that ushered him in restored the years her bitterness had stolen as the spring rain creates new birth from the barrenness of winter.

Gomer's walking stick fell from her hand and clattered against the flagstones of the kitchen floor.

271

Historical Background

c. 1020–722 B.C.

The countdown to Israel's zero hour began with the cry, "Give us a king like all the other nations have" (1 Sam. 8:5). God's heart was pierced when His children wanted a new king. His love was such that He would not desert them, though they turned against Him. He was always there in the hopes that they would throw their spiritual arms around Him and return. He had sent them prophets, but they spurned or even killed them (Matt. 23:37).

The twelve tribes were united in the days of their first king, Saul. The one true God was on their side and His children, Israel, were safe from the surrounding countries forever, because they were obedient in following all the laws and sacrifices exactly as Moses had given, or so they thought.

God's chosen had never really understood the purpose of the sacrifice (Jer. 7:22–24). To some it was no different from the appeasements the heathen made to *their* idols. So they sacrificed, but it was often only a bribe offered to God, and then to the false gods for good measure. God's children never realized that He loved them. To them, El Shaddai was no different from other gods, only mightier (Jer. 2:27–28).

After Saul, God sent them David, the king that slew his ten thousands. But now the smell of blood was in Israel's nostrils. Because God had sent them to war for the land of Canaan in Joshua's time, about 650 years before Hosea, they must have assumed God approved this way of life. They heightened their power by conquering and spread their boundaries with blood. Their wealth increased and they embraced the gods of their booty. But that was all right, they thought, as long as they did not forget to sacrifice to the Lord God also (Jer. 7:8-10).

With King Solomon the wealth and fame of Israel reached a new plateau. But the king known for his wisdom enforced a heavy yoke, and when he died the people demanded that his son, Rehoboam, lighten the hard service of his father (1 Ki. 12:4).

When Rehoboam refused, ten of the tribes of Israel rebelled, making Jeroboam I (a man who was not of the royal line of David) their new king (1 Ki. 12:16,20). The rebellion caused the house of Israel to divide: Judah in southern Canaan and Israel in the north. The second step of their calamity was completed; the family was torn.

From this time on Israel's history reads like the downward slope of a roller coaster, leveling off at points, momentarily gaining a short uphill stroke, but always losing altitude in the end, gaining momentum as it headed for the bottom.

Half a century after King Jeroboam I, a man named Ahab became ruler of Israel. He was the most wicked king in Hebrew history. His wife Jezebel wrought more evil than her husband, who encouraged the worship of Baal (1 Ki. 16:31-32). God used Jehu to wipe out the family of Ahab (2 Ki. 9:6-7) but this king was bloodthirsty (2 Ki. 9:33-34). He was not content only to take the throne from Ahab's descendants, but indulged in a murderous spree that caused men to tremble in obedience to his every word. He slaughtered everyone remotely connected to Ahab, even by friendship, and murdered every Baal-worshiper in the land. God rewarded him for taking the throne from the family of Ahab with the promise that his sons to the fourth generation would reign over Israel (2 Ki. 10:1-30).

Jehu's son Jehoahaz was wicked, but he later entreated the Lord on behalf of Israel, and God listened. The Lord sent Israel a deliverer so they could escape the oppression from the Syrians, and the sons of Israel lived in their tents as before, apparently as a sign of returning to God as in the days of their desert roaming. Yet they still did not give up their sins of idolatry begun in the reign of Jeroboam I. The Lord was particularly jealous of the Asherah (a wooden symbol of a female deity that King Ahab made) that remained standing in Samaria (2 Ki. 13:1-6).

Toward the end of King Jehoahaz's reign other neighboring countries, besides the Syrians, were becoming bolder. In the spring of the year bands of Moabites (to the east of Israel) roved the land in search of plunder. They terrorized the tent people and village dwellers for years (2 Ki. 13:20-22).

Still, God didn't turn His back on Israel because of His covenant with Abraham, Isaac, and Jacob. El Shaddai, God Almighty, tried yet again to woo them back by delivering them. When Hazael died (the king of Syria who had taken many cities from Jehoahaz), his son Ben-hadad became king in his place. Then Joash, the son of Jehoahaz, fought and won all the cities back from Ben-hadad (2 Ki. 13:24-25).

During the reign of Joash, King Amaziah of Judah challenged Israel to war. King Joash haughtily warned him that Judah couldn't stand against him, but Amaziah insisted. They warred and Judah lost. Israel tore down the wall of Jerusalem from the gate of Ephraim to the Corner Gate and then plundered the city and the temple (2 Ki. 14:8-14). God's chosen people were fighting among themselves. Surely their downfall was not far off.

Up and down went Israel's power. Back and forth went their boundaries. The power of the Syrians was a constant thorn in Israel's side, but little did they realize that the sleeping giant Assyria, to the north, was their real threat.

When Jeroboam II, the son of Joash, became king he did evil in the sight of God. But he was mighty in battle, and in fulfillment of prophecy, further restored the borders of Israel that had been slowly closing in over the last century. Jeroboam recovered from Judah the coveted Damascus and the city of Hamath (2 Ki. 14:23-28).

During the forty-one years of Jeroboam's reign, Samaria, the capital of Israel, reached the apex of its splendor. In a great show of Israel's invincibility (and possibly their fear) Jeroboam refortified the city with a great double wall. At its most exposed sections this wall spread as wide as thirty-three feet, and so sturdy was it that twenty-four years after his reign, it took three years of siege for the Assyrians to break through (2 Ki. 17:5).

The capital city housed the palace, resplendent with its limestone walls, rooms of ivory, and glorious outer courts. Above all soared a strong rectangular tower like a never-sleeping sentry. Because Jeroboam II seemed to bring Jehovah's blessing to Israel through such prosperity, it can be assumed that he was beloved of the people. When he died a number of years elapsed before his son Zechariah was king. This fulfilled God's promise to Jehu that, "Your sons to the fourth generation shall sit on the throne of Israel."

Zechariah also did evil, but apparently accomplished

nothing else. This was probably due to the fact that he was assassinated by a usurper named Shallum only six months after he was enthroned. Israel was in such a state of anarchy at this time that Shallum actually murdered Zechariah publically and no one made a move to stop him; on the contrary, he became king (2 Ki. 15:10).

Shallum reigned for one month. When Menahem, the general of Jeroboam's army, heard of Shallum's coup, he came up from the city of Tirzah and struck down Shallum to become king himself. He ruled in savage power, and his reign of ten years proved his strength, as this length of kingship was somewhat of a record for his time (2 Ki. 15:13–22).

This bloody battle for power played itself out before ten apparently apathetic tribes of Israel. There is no mention of anyone, save Amos and Hosea, attempting to stop it.

During Menahem's rule he was forced to buy off the Assyrians to be Israel's ally (2 Ki. 15:19). As Hosea says, "Ephraim has hired lovers, they hire allies among the nations . . . " (Hos. 8:9–10).

It is in the last year of Jeroboam II's reign that the story of Hosea and Gomer begins. When Jeroboam dies (and no one is sure how), the Syrians are beginning the final and fullest burst of power in their history, only to fail in conquering Israel and fall to Assyria ten years before Israel.

The eighth century B.C. saw Israel at the height of prosperity. But haughtiness, immorality, selfishness, idolatry, greed, and treachery were also at a height. This was the other side of the picture of power and luxury, and it was a horrid sketch of oppression of the poor and helpless (Amos 4:1). The wealthy had become rich from the spoils of war. They used their wealth to buy up the land until the poor had to rent land that was once theirs to farm and graze (Amos 5:11).

If a commoner found he was being cheated, he quickly learned it was futile to take the rich to court; the judges took bribes (Amos 5:12). To make matters worse, the poor were in constant danger of the Moabites or some other marauding tribe, who burned their fields. When a commoner was unable to pay rent on the land, the rich landowner took him or his children as slaves to work off the debt. There was no escape for the poor, and there was no limit to what the rich could get by with.

The prophet Amos spoke against these social atrocities during the reign of Jeroboam II. No one listened. With all the blessings bestowed on Israel, the people thought they must be pleasing God. If they weren't then God must be dead, for He did not take away the blessing as a sign of His displeasure. Either way, the rich were satisfied, and the poor were pacified.

Hosea's story is set against this backdrop of raging injustice. Moral depravity and perversion had sunk to its lowest depth in Israel's history. Maybe it is only against such a dark environment that God's love can shine brilliantly enough for us to see it. Amos and Hosea were the two prophets God sent to Israel during this dark hour. Amos preached social reform, and although Hosea addressed this issue, his primary aim was to plead with Israel to return to God and receive the personal love He yearned to give. Hosea was the first to introduce the astounding concept of the Lord God as a loving, self-sacrificing husband.

Hosea has been called the prophet of a broken heart, and his living example of God's love to Israel and the heartache God endured from His people was a blatant, hard-hitting message, shown through Hosea's marriage to Gomer the harlot. Such a message was needed to pierce the thick heads and hearts of the Israelites. The land cried out, "My God, we of Israel know thee!" but they lied (Hos. 8:2 NKJV). They rebelled against God's law; they transgressed His covenant.

Israel could not know God, for so integrated was idolatry into their worship that their conception of the Lord God was no different than of other gods (Hos. 5:4). Their sacrifices and rituals had come to be only an appeasement to God so that they could still believe they were in His favor.

Is that so different from the conception many have today of God? Do we need such an agonizing example to get through to us? We have the Book of Hosea. But as with the Israelites of the eighth century, will this glorious truth go unheeded? If our understanding of God's divine love and mercy is changed to that of Hosea's, then he did not endure such heartbreak in vain.

For the country of Israel, Hosea's prophetic voice was the beginning of the last call—a call to which they did not hearken. More than one hundred years before Judah fell, in the year 722 B.C. Assyria invaded Israel. The ten tribes of Israel were no more (2 Ki. 17:20).